Turning Point in China

Turning Point in China

an essay on the
Cultural Revolution
by William Hinton

(MR) New York and London

Contents

Author's Note

This essay is based on a lecture I gave before various American university audiences in 1970–1971. In the spring of 1971 I returned to China for the first time since 1953. What I learned during seven months of travel and interviews, while enriching and deepening my understanding of the Cultural Revolution, basically confirmed the account given in these pages.

I am indebted to Martin Davis of the Brooklyn Polytechnical Institute and to Hassan Zavareei for taping my lectures at the New School for Social Research and for transcribing them in a form which made this writing possible.

Chapter 1

Class Struggle Under Socialism

The Great Proletarian Cultural Revolution in China may well be the most important political development of the second half of the twentieth century. As a turning point in history it can be compared with the Russian Revolution of 1917. Ever since the Russian working class, led by Lenin, seized state power more than fifty years ago, world politics has been in essence action and reaction around that event. Now, when the Russian working class has lost power to a resurgent bourgeoisie, and socialism in the first workers' state has degenerated into social imperialism, the Chinese working class, led by Mao Tse-tung, is smashing the challenge of a resurgent bourgeoisie in its own country and carrying the socialist revolution forward to a new stage. As this movement progresses, world politics will increasingly revolve around it and China will stand at the center of the world stage for a time just as the Soviet Union did from 1917 to 1956.

The victory won by the Chinese people in 1949, important as it was to the balance of class power in the world, cannot be evaluated in the same terms as the Russian Revolution. In 1949 Chinese workers, allied with the peasants, the urban petty bourgeoisie, and elements of the capitalist class seized power and began the socialist transformation of their land. But since the Russian people had earlier pio-

9

neered the socialist road, this was not an historic break-through; it was rather the continuation and extension of the October Revolution already thirty years old.

By 1966, however, a whole new situation had arisen in the world. Socialist revolutions, though they had succeeded in transforming the economic base in a number of countries, had failed to solve the problem of bourgeois restoration. With the consciousness of the people only partially remolded, and the superstructure of society only partially recast, working class power had already been subverted in Russia and most of Eastern Europe and was under serious challenge everywhere else. At this critical juncture, the Chinese working class and its Communist Party went on the offensive. "Taking the upset of the cart in front as a warning to the cart behind," they launched a tremendous struggle to expose and defeat revisionist forces inside China and reverse the course these forces had imposed on much of the country.

Without any beaten path to follow, without any tested theory to light their way, China's revolutionaries now stand at the cutting edge of history—much as the Bolsheviks did in Moscow and Petrograd after 1917. Whether or not they are able to consolidate power and carry the socialist revolution forward where others have failed is of crucial importance not only to the Chinese people, but to the anti-imperialist struggle of all the oppressed peoples and to the revolutionary struggle of all exploited classes. Whoever doubts this should try to imagine the world without a powerful socialist state to confront and expose both imperialism and social imperialism, to give aid to national liberation struggles, to pioneer in building a new society free from exploitation and oppression. Clearly this is a turning point, not only for China but for the rest of the world.

Truth, it has been said, is always revolutionary. No exception to this rule, the truth about the Cultural Revolution is full of surprises. Most of the theories that circulate in the West fall far short of explaining the basic forces in conflict, much less the twists and turns of the developing struggle. Revolutions are rooted in crisis, but the Cultural Revolution, despite the alarums sounded by so many China watchers, did not evolve out of social, political, or economic crises in the usual sense. China was not, for instance, facing any economic impasse in 1966 when the upheaval began. The Chinese economy had been growing steadily for a number of years, crops had been good, and industrial output had been rising. A number of foreign economists had predicted that the country was on the eve of further rapid industrial development. In fact, this very healthy progress and growth potential was one reason for the Cultural Revolution taking place when it did. When any economy is on the verge of expansion it is important to the class forces in command that the direction be clear. To be specific, in the case of China, it was important both to Mao and his supporters and to the opposition whether the country's huge economic potential was to develop in a socialist or a capitalist direction. China's economic health, then, was a cogent reason for the issues to come into the open when they did.

That China's economy was doing well in the sixties is confirmed by a number of rather extraordinary facts. First, China continued to feed, clothe, equip, and care for its growing population at rising per-capita rates while comparable countries such as India struggled from one crisis to another. There is no way to prove this statistically—statistics have not generally been available since 1959—but the observations of numerous foreign visitors who, taken collectively, traveled the length and breadth of the land in the years preceding the Cultural Revolution, add up to a picture of stability and prosperity both rural and urban. Second, prices had remained stable in China for seventeen years. In fact, since 1949 many prices in China had fallen. Throughout the whole period of socialist construction after the Communist Party took power the Chinese dollar was among the soundest in the world—one of the few currencies not subject to the general inflation which wracked most economies east and west. Third, after paying off all debts to the Soviet Union in the middle sixties, the Chinese government carried no debt, either internal or external. China owed nothing to any foreign government or banker, nor did China owe anything to any internal bank or individual. This is something unique in today's world.

Crises, of course, can be external as well as internal. Some observers, Han Suyin for one, have stressed the mounting military threat from American imperialism in the Pacific and Southeast Asia and from Soviet social imperialism in Siberia as decisive in forcing a realignment in China. From this standpoint the Cultural Revolution is interpreted as an effort to put one's house in order in preparation for massive external attack.

Certainly one cannot deny that such a threat existed or that it was mounting in scale and intensity. Certainly issues of foreign policy were important in the Cultural Revolution. Differences over how to handle the rising threat of American imperialism, the growing collaboration between America and the USSR and the sharpening quarrel with the USSR over border problems and world policy; differences over how to develop modern defensive armaments; differences over support for national liberation struggles: all came to a head after 1966 and helped to define the dividing line between the contending forces in China. But it would be wrong to consider rising external pressure as the source of these differences or as the prime cause of the Cultural Revolution as a whole. The Cultural Revolution developed as a result of internal contradictions, as a result of clashes of interest and ideology arising out of the socialist construction of China and the stage which that construction had reached. Differences over foreign policy likewise had their source in these internal contradictions. Concrete analysis of the socialist revolution inside China is needed in order to understand what happened.

In general, the American academic world does view the Cultural Revolution as a clash of internal forces, but within this overall context some very inadequate theses have been postulated. One of these is that Mao Tse-tung arranged the Cultural Revolution in order to test and train all revolutionary cadres and especially those students of the new generation who had no firsthand experience of class struggle, civil war, or international war. In other words, no real struggle went on in China at all but only a kind of shadow play arranged by Mao for the education of his followers. The same people who promote this view are particularly vehement on the subject of voluntarism. They claim that history and human nature have a character of their own which cannot be tampered with by individuals. They claim that Mao is a utopian dreamer who is trying to impose his will on intractable human and social reality, an exercise in futility that only a revolutionary fanatic would undertake. At the same time they claim that Mao has singlehandedly thrown China into six years of extraordinary turmoil involving hundreds of millions of people in intense political activity that has wrecked the economy, wrecked the Communist Party, and endangered the future of the nation.

Is there not a contradiction here? One cannot have it both ways. One cannot claim that individual will is powerless to change history and man and at the same time assert that Mao has by an act of will changed both history and man. This theory hardly needs further refutation. The academicians are hoist on their own petard, or, as the Chinese would say, "they have lifted a rock only to drop it on their own feet."

A more widely circulated theory of the Cultural Revolution is that it is a struggle over succession. That is, Mao Tse-tung is old and will die within a reasonable period, or so these theorists hope, and the question that has been agitating China is: Who will succeed Mao? According to this theory the upheaval of the Cultural Revolution is nothing more than the jockeying of various factions behind various individuals who hope to seize supreme power.

But where has there ever been a struggle for political power between personalities unconnected with deeper issues of politics? Positions of influence and power are sought for class reasons, to promote the interests of one class against another, one section of a class against another section, one vested interest against another. There is no such thing as abstract "struggle for power," struggle between personalities in a social and political vacuum.

An example of this "vacuum" theory is Chalmers Johnson's *Peasant Nationalism and Communist Power.** This book discusses the role of revolutionary Communists in Yugoslavia and China, especially during World War II

---

* *Peasant Nationalism and Communist Power: The Emergence of a Revolutionary China, 1937–1945* (Stanford, Calif.: Stanford University Press, 1962).

when Communists won unchallenged leadership of the national liberation struggle in those two countries. Johnson's concept is of a China that contained two rootless elites, the Kuomintang clique headed by Chiang Kai-shek and the Communist clique headed by Mao Tse-tung. Both cliques sought power in China, apparently for power's sake, and they contended with each other for this prize. When all is said and done, the only reason why Mao won out over Chiang was that Mao was smarter. Confronted with an all-out Japanese attack, Mao handled the national question more skillfully, armed the masses, organized the liberation of vast areas, and won enormous prestige—so says Johnson.

But is that really the essence of the matter? Did Mao win out over Chiang simply by thinking straighter? After all, Chiang Kai-shek was undoubtedly a very brilliant man. Furthermore, even if he could not think straight, in 1937 he controlled most of the wealth of China. He could have hired professors from Chinese universities or even from American universities to map out a resistance program for the embattled Chinese nation. If that did not work he could have stolen a page from Mao Tse-tung's book and learned from him how to arm and lead the masses. If he really only wanted power why didn't he do that? He didn't do it because he did not seek power for power's sake but to protect the interests of the Chinese landed gentry, whom he represented, to maintain his hold on the enormous wealth which he had expropriated as a bureaucrat in power, and to serve the American and British imperial interests whose military and financial support enabled him to seize power in the first place. Arming the masses was not compatible with any of these goals because the masses, once armed and having settled accounts with Japan, would inevitably move against landed gentry, bureaucratic capitalists, and American and British imperialists. Chiang Kai-shek, far from being rootless, had deep roots in everything that was reactionary, oppressive, and doomed in China. There was no way that he could lead the national liberation struggle of the Chinese people to a successful conclusion.

Another example of "vacuum" theory is a recent *China Quarterly* article that explains the Cultural Revolution as a personal struggle between Lin Piao, Minister of Defense, and P'eng Chen, former mayor of Peking. Lin Piao, it seems, won out by a really clever strategy: he flattered Mao all the time.* He went around speaking in favor of Mao and his line, quoted Mao and applauded Mao. Mao consequently relied on him and placed him in line for the succession. But if P'eng Chen only wanted the position of chairman of the Chinese Communist Party, if Mao had the power to hand this out to whoever pleased him most, and if Mao was so easily flattered, why didn't P'eng Chen go around making speeches in favor of Mao's line, quoting Mao and applauding Mao, and thus steal a march on Lin Piao? This whole framework is childish and obscurantist in the extreme. One can only come to ridiculous conclusions when one tries to analyze major political developments apart from class analysis, apart from the class struggle and the national struggle that goes on in the real world.

The heart of the Cultural Revolution has indeed been a struggle for power, a struggle over the control of state power in China, who is going to hold it, who is going to wield it, that is, which individual people. But it has not been a struggle over power for power's sake; rather, a strug-

---

* Lin Piao's ascendancy did not last very long. It seems clear now (December 1971) that his political career has ended.

gle between individuals representing conflicting class interests. It has been a class struggle to determine whether individuals representing the working class or individuals representing the bourgeoisie will hold state power. It has been a struggle to determine whether China will continue to take the socialist road and carry the socialist revolution through to the end, or whether China will abandon the socialist road for the capitalist road. That is why the struggle has been so sharp. That is why all the democratic forms worked out in the socialist period for debating issues and for choosing people for positions of power have proved inadequate to resolve the conflict. Historically, basic issues of class power the world over have never been settled by discussions and elections, but instead have been settled on the battlefield.

Within a year after the Cultural Revolution began, rather severe fighting did break out in various parts of China. It became serious enough to be called by Mao "all-round civil war." The only reason it did not escalate into large-scale armed conflict on a classic pattern was that the People's Liberation Army, in the main, remained under the control of Mao Tse-tung, Lin Piao, and the proletarian headquarters. Attempts on the part of bourgeois forces to seize arms and take over military units were generally foiled. In this situation Mao was able to carry out a massive mobilization of the people for political rather than armed struggle, and thus a contradiction between the people and their enemies began to be resolved by methods generally used for resolving conflicts among the people—i.e., political methods.

To explain the Cultural Revolution in terms of class struggle over state power between the working class and the bourgeoisie puzzles people. Many immediately ask: Wasn't that question settled in 1949? After all, what was the great Chinese Revolution all about? Wasn't there a working class party, the Chinese Communist Party? And wasn't there an army led by this party? And didn't this party and this army lead the whole people in smashing the old regime and setting up a new state that carried through socialist transformation? Obviously the working class came to power in 1949, after smashing the power of the big bourgeoisie allied with feudalism. True, some national capitalists joined the Communist-led struggle, but they were weak, they had no armed forces of their own. How could they challenge the working class for control of China seventeen years later?

The answer to this is that the revolution that culminated in victory in 1949 was not a socialist revolution. Although led by the working class and its party, the targets of the time were feudalism (landlordism) internally and imperialism externally. Bureaucratic capitalism was added to these targets as the fortunes of the Chiang-Kung-Soong-Ch'en puppet clique grew, but capitalism as such, private enterprise as such, never was the target. The victory of 1949 smashed landlord and bureaucratic capitalist power in China and drove the imperialists out. It thereby opened the road for socialist transformation. It also opened the road for ordinary capitalist development. Which road China would eventually take was not determined by that victory alone. Much depended upon how the Communist Party, how the Chinese people, and how the various classes in the anti-feudal, anti-imperialist alliance handled the new situation. The contradiction of the Chinese people versus the feudal landlords, bureaucratic capitalists, and imperialists had been resolved; but the contradiction of the Chinese people versus the bourgeoisie, the heart of which was working class versus bourgeoisie, immediately took its place. Right away a struggle began inside and outside the Party over how to handle this contradiction, and the two poles of opinion and organization which arose represented two distinct roads for China—the capitalist road and the socialist road. Clearly this question was not solved in 1949.

But, many people will say, if it was not solved in 1949 surely it was solved by 1957. During that eight-year period China's whole economy underwent a transformation. The small holdings which peasants seized as a result of land reform were pooled into cooperatives and then into collectives of a socialist nature. Individual and small-scale handicraft industries also joined together into socialist cooperatives. The private industrial and commercial holdings of the national bourgeoisie were turned over to the state at various levels in return for government bonds bearing interest at 5 percent and thus became socialist property. Simultaneously the huge holdings confiscated from the bureaucratic capitalists in 1949 developed as the socialist center of gravity of the whole system. By 1957 China was clearly a socialist and no longer a new democratic country. Private property in the means of production had been done away with. How then could a struggle over state power arise between the working class and the bourgeoisie almost ten years later?

The answer to that is that the socialist transformation of an economy is only the first step in a socialist revolution. It is a very important step but it is not, by itself, decisive. In order to consolidate socialism the working class must not only transform the economic base of society but also the whole superstructure. The ideology, culture, customs, and habits of the people must be transformed along with all the institutions that reflect and perpetuate them such as schools, religious organizations, trade unions, peasant associations, theater companies, orchestras, publishing houses, and scientific bodies. New music, art, literature, and drama must be created that is working class in content. Furthermore, each individual must conduct an internal struggle to replace bourgeois individualism with proletarian collectivism as his or her motivating thought. Unless all this is carried through the socialist economic base cannot be consolidated.

Socialism is after all not something given, something fixed. It is a process, a transition from one stage of society to another. Just as capitalism must be regarded as a transition from feudalism to socialism, so socialism must be regarded as a transition from capitalism to communism (or in the case of China from new democracy to communism). As such it bears within it many contradictions, many inequalities that cannot be done away with overnight or even in the course of several years or several decades. These inequalities are inherited from the old society, such things as pay differentials between skilled and unskilled work and between mental and manual work, such things as differences between the economic, educational, and cultural opportunities available in the city and in the countryside, such things as bourgeois right, which includes such concepts as equality in the market place, equality in voting, and equality before the law when in fact people of unequal means can never be equal in the market place, in voting, in court, or anywhere else. It is impossible at one stroke to cut the pay of skilled workers to that of the unskilled or to raise the pay of the unskilled to skilled levels. It is impossible at one stroke to reduce the earnings of intellectuals to the level of rank-and-file bench-workers or to raise the pay of bench-workers to a par with that of intellectuals. It is impossible at one stroke to make country living as rich and varied as city living, to provide the same quality of education, recreation, social life, medical care, etc., throughout the vast countryside as is taken for granted in the cities. Yet as long as these inequalities exist they generate privilege, individualism, careerism, and bourgeois ideology. Without a conscious and protracted effort to combat these tendencies they can grow into an important social force. They can and do create new bourgeois individuals who gather as a new privileged elite and ultimately as a new exploiting class. Thus socialism can be peacefully transformed back into capitalism.

Clearly class struggle continues throughout the period of socialism. It continues as long as classes exist, as long as classes are generated, and there is no such thing as putting an end to this struggle by simply collectivizing the economy, or even by carrying through a cultural revolution.

There is no such thing as putting a quick end to the struggle, but there is such a thing as winning the protracted war against bourgeois restoration through a conscious revolutionary effort to mobilize the mass of the people for whom socialism is the only way out. By consolidating working class rule and seizing back power wherever it has been usurped, the superstructure and the economic base can be transformed, and individual consciousness can be transformed so that inequality, bourgeois right, and the bourgeois ideology which they generate are blocked, cut back, and finally eliminated when the class forces that generate them are eliminated.

So the question of the capitalist road versus the socialist road was not settled in China in 1949, nor was it settled in 1956. Nor has it been finally settled by the Cultural Revolution even though at this time the working class is on the way to an important victory. Mao Tse-tung has pointed out that there will and must be successive cultural revolutions in the future and that the question of which class will ultimately rule and which road will ultimately be followed can only be settled after decades, perhaps centuries of political struggle. This estimate of Mao's is based on the history of the class struggle in the past, on the history of the capitalist challenge to feudalism which lasted for at least two hundred years, and which in many areas of the world is still going on today. Anti-feudal forces cut off the king's head more than once, only to find a new king restored to power. In the bourgeois period revolution and counter-revolution engaged in seesaw battle throughout the world for a long time and yet the conflict between the landed gentry and the rising business and commercial classes was by no means as sharp as that between the working class and the bourgeoisie today. For all that happened during the bourgeois revolution was the replacement of one form of private property by another. Power based on the ownership and control of land was replaced by power based on the ownership and control of industrial capital and in the process at least some of the landed elite transferred a portion of their wealth from land to industrial capital, while numerous compromises were worked out which maintained private property in land and served as a drag and brake on the development of "free private enterprise." The socialist revolution goes far deeper than this. The working class, in order to liberate itself, must end all private ownership of the means of production and prevent its restoration through transforming the ideology of the people and this is a much more difficult task than that undertaken by the bourgeoisie. It would be very naive to think that such a task will be easier to accomplish than that which preceded it. No, the socialist revolution will take a long, long time and must expect many twists, turns, and setbacks.

Chapter 2

The Class Forces

The class struggle continued in China throughout the fifties and in the middle sixties came to a head in a new form in a society that already had an advancing socialist economy, and already had made some progress in the socialist transformation of the superstructure. In order to understand the course of this struggle it is important to understand what bourgeois class forces actually existed in China after 1956 that could challenge the working class for power.

First we will take up the obvious ones. The traditional national bourgeoisie whose holdings were bought out by the People's Government in the fifties still survived in the sixties. As a class they no longer held any important position of power in the economy or in the state structure. Nevertheless, as individuals they carried on, and their special relationship to the means of production was evidenced by the fact that they still drew interest on the government bonds which they had been given in exchange for their industrial and commercial holdings.* Some of them still worked as managers in the companies they used to own. Others worked as technicians. They did not constitute a

---

* This may be an exception to the previous generalization about internal debt, since these bonds were a form of state debt. My understanding is that since 1966 interest payments have not been drawn.

major threat to socialism, in part because many of them had accepted socialist remolding as necessary and in part because everyone knew who they were and discounted them politically and ideologically. At the same time, it seems clear that they represented a bourgeois stratum of some importance.

Much more important were the many bourgeois intellectuals who staffed much of the educational system, most of the professions, and many state institutions. Most of China's modern intellectuals were bourgeois if not landlord in class origin and bourgeois in training. Many of them were simultaneously revolutionary. They hated and had long hated Chinese feudalism and the various imperialist conquerors of China. Large numbers had long advocated not simply national liberation but socialism, and not a few had become Communist Party members. But as Mao Tse-tung often stressed, it takes at least ten years of education and participation in sharp class struggle to transform a bourgeois intellectual into a proletarian revolutionary. Many had not been systematically re-educated, many had not taken part in years of class struggle, and some who had been so educated and involved had not been thoroughly proletarianized by the experience. Large numbers of intellectuals had simply been absorbed into the revolutionary camp through the process of liberation by the People's Liberation Army and they had carried on more or less as usual in spite of numerous campaigns to retrain them and redirect their work.

Intellectuals play an extraordinary role in China, partly because there are so few of them. Their influence spreads far out of proportion to their numbers. They are particularly important in the arts and sciences, of course, and the revolution cannot get along without them. Nevertheless as long as they have not been remolded, they spread bour-

geois ideology and bourgeois practice into every intellectual sphere, and, what is equally important, train up a
younger generation in their own image. The class struggle
under socialism amounts to the bourgeoisie trying to remold the world to suit themselves while the working class
tries to remold the world to suit working people. For a
time, particularly in the cultural field, the bourgeoisie has
a distinct advantage, a built-in advantage, because most of
the positions and most of the reputations belong to them
and the working class needs them to pass on the accumulated knowledge and skills of the past.

If there were no mass base for bourgeois ideology this
might not be so important, but in fact, among the peasantry there remained a mass base for just such ideas. To
some extent all of China's peasants, as petty owners of
productive property, were carriers of bourgeois ideology.
But I am talking here about those former rich, upper-middle, and middle peasants who, though they had been absorbed into the communes, still retained illusions about
the capitalist road; peasants who privately thought that if
only the collective economy were not so strong they could
prosper in a dog-eat-dog competitive race. Such people
were constantly putting private interest foremost and
pushing for bigger private plots, expanded free markets,
the right to buy-and-sell, peddle, and speculate, and the
right to produce as families rather than as teams or brigades in a mutually dependent collective.

After land reform one such family drew up a five-year
plan which was conspicuously lacking in socialist content.
They planned to work hard the first year, save and buy
seed and tools so that the second year after much hard
work they could afford a draft animal. With the help of
the animal they hoped to earn enough the third year to
buy more land and finally, with the fourth year's accumu-

lation, hire an extra hand. Obviously if some buy land others must sell. If some hire help others must hire out. Only a few can go up. Most must sink down. Such is the capitalist road. Nevertheless a percentage of former rich peasants and middle peasants still had illusions that they personally would go up. Even if this percentage was small it must be taken on a base of several hundred million people. Certainly there must have been in China tens of millions of peasants who had not entirely rejected the capitalist road and would have welcomed any lead given by the more strategically placed intellectuals whether it be in the field of culture, economics, or politics. These "capitalist roaders" among the peasantry then could and often did sway masses of poor and lower-middle peasants in the direction of immediate self-interest, to the detriment of long-range collective interests.

Such were the obvious bourgeois forces in China's socialist society seventeen years after the start of the socialist revolution. There were other forces that were not so obvious. One of these was the new managerial and administrative elite thrown up by the revolution itself, revolutionaries who had come to power after 1949 and had been corrupted by the influence they wielded and the privileges they had thereby been able to seize. Vice-manager Li, of Chiheng State Farm, was one such person whom I personally knew. He was not only vice-manager of a large state farm in southern Hopei Province, but was the secretary of its Communist Party organization. He came from Nankung, a commercial center on the North China plain, and had absorbed buying-and-selling with his mother's milk. Using capital allotted to the farm for seed and fertilizer he expanded a small cooperative that originally supplied towels and toothpaste to the farm's workers into a large wholesale business that marketed cigarettes far and wide. Some of the capital that accrued from this commerce was spent on a cotton gin that processed government-owned cotton on a piecework basis. Not satisfied with the normal returns for such work, Secretary Li led his staff in substituting off-grade cotton for the good cotton supplied by the state. Then they sold the prime fiber elsewhere. Though some of the income was reported to the state to show how profitable the farm had become, another portion was privately expropriated and spent on high living. Campaigns such as the Three-Anti and Five-Anti movements of 1952 helped expose and remove corrupt cadres like Li, but the new socialist society continued to generate them nevertheless and some succeeded in building rather extensive "kingdoms" where likeminded individuals provided mutual support and protection for very questionable practices.

Alongside these corrupt elements stood those sincere revolutionaries of the new democratic period who had never really turned the corner of the socialist revolution. They had fought hard to overthrow feudal power and to drive imperialism out of China, they talked about socialism, even dreamed about socialism, but when socialism actually came on the agenda they hesitated or were frightened. Mao Tse-tung compared such cadre to Lord Shih, who loved dragons. This legendary figure collected pictures of dragons and statues of dragons but when a live dragon came down the road he ran away as fast as he could. An editorial during the Cultural Revolution had this to say: "Many of our Party members date back to the days of the democratic revolutionary struggle. When they were faced with the new socialist revolution the fighting will of some of them broke. Others did not understand the meaning of the socialist revolution and while they thought they were engaged in socialism, it turned out that they were engaged in capitalism." Such people had long been nothing more than petty-bourgeois revolutionaries. One could call them unconscious revisionists.

Much more formidable were the conscious revisionists, those leading Communist cadre who consciously revised basic Marxist principles concerning the persistence of class struggle in the socialist period, the dialectical relationship between base and superstructure, and the difference between revolution and modernization. These people accepted Khrushchev's theories of peaceful coexistence, peaceful competition, and peaceful transition, and tried to lead China down the economic road systematized by the Soviet economist Y. G. Lieberman. They opposed each basic process of the socialist transformation of China and when difficulties arose on any front urged abandonment of socialist institutions and norms altogether. Some of them, including Liu Shao-ch'i, who headed this faction, had been oppositionists in the new democratic period, pursuing policies that laid the groundwork for capitalism rather than socialism after the defeat of Chiang Kai-shek and imperialism. Liu's clique formed a bourgeois headquarters inside the Chinese Communist Party that mobilized, organized, and led all the other conscious and unconscious bourgeois forces in city and countryside.

Actually all three of the above mentioned categories of cadre were part of the group that Mao Tse-tung called "Party people in authority taking the capitalist road," and all of them were targets of attack in the Cultural Revolution. A distinction was made, however, between those who took the capitalist road by mistake, because of a low level of political consciousness, personal selfishness, etc., and those diehard capitalist roaders who consciously opposed socialism and socialist revolution. The former could usually be won over and reformed after being criticized and educated by the masses. Their mistakes were considered to fall within the category of "contradictions among the people," and were treated by the method of "curing the disease and saving the patient." The latter, as a conscious counter-revolutionary force, were treated as enemies of the people, and though they too were given a way out as individuals—that is a chance to recognize their wrong road, to reform, and to take up new work—their cases were much more serious because, as leading Communists, they were in a position to mobilize and lead all the bourgeois forces back to power. In fact under the conditions existing in socialist China they were the only group in a position to do so. They were the ideological and organizational center for the bourgeoisie as a class.

Standing behind these bourgeois forces, always ready to move as the struggle sharpened, were the remnant landlord elements who numbered in the millions. While they made up only 2 or 3 percent of old China they still totaled close to 20,000,000 individuals. Most of them survived the revolution. They lost their land, received only a share equal to that of any poor peasant, and had to go to work on it to live. Most of them hated work, hated the new society and waited only for a chance to turn the clock back. An issue of the *New York Times Magazine* in 1970 told the story of one Red Guard rebel who later fled to Taiwan. During the Cultural Revolution he headed a violent, ultra-left uprising in his mainland school. His real goal, he later admitted, had been to overthrow the Communist regime and reclaim his family's estate. Such people lurked in the wings all over China, along with expropriated compradores, their erstwhile retainers, remnants of the underworld gangs of Shanghai, Tientsin, and Canton, and other criminal and lumpen elements. Backing them up from abroad were the imperialists, especially the Americans astride Taiwan. They constantly sent in agents, probed for weak spots, and brandished atomic weapons as a threat toward all who might persist in revolution. Soviet revisionists, on their part, made contact with the revisionist elements in Party leadership, gave them all possible moral and political support, and joined the international chorus of those who warned against provoking imperialism lest it destroy the world.

All of this adds up to a formidable anti-socialist force, backed up by reactionary feudal and criminal elements and supported from abroad by the most powerful states in the world.

The center of gravity, the crucial element in this whole complex was, as stated above, made up of those conscious revisionists, the diehard class enemies among the "Party people in authority taking the capitalist road." American analysts and scholars have gone to great lengths to show that these people, the main targets of attack in the Cultural Revolution, did not constitute a headquarters, an organized group, but were simply a collection of isolated individuals who, for one reason or another, fell out of favor with their colleagues, with their students, or with Mao Tse-tung and his "clique."

In the main, so American analysts aver, these conscious "capitalist roaders" were nothing but pragmatists, political and economic realists who were trying their best with the human material and resources at hand to modernize China and develop it into a great industrial and military power worthy of consideration alongside the United States and the USSR. Mao and his supporters, on the other hand, are presented as dogmatists, revolutionary fanatics who were trying to impose utopian ideas of equality and selflessness on ordinary selfish human beings, and by this effort were destroying China's economy, dragging China down into the mud and betraying the interests of the Chinese people.

This is all very curious, because, knowing the American ruling class, we know that one thing they very much fear is a strong, united, industrialized China—a China that is in fact a great power. Since this is what they really fear and since Mao, according to their theories, is leading China to disaster, they ought to close ranks behind Mao and give him full support so that China can never develop into a serious threat to the world ambitions of the United States. Instead, they have closed ranks behind Liu Shao-ch'i, the pragmatist, the practical, hardworking politician who has the kind of policy and plan that can make China a great power. Is there not something fundamentally specious here?

To the American ruling class Liu Shao-ch'i's revisionism is simply common sense while Mao Tse-tung's socialist road is irrational. This should give us all pause for thought. To the bourgeoisie any demand for working class power, any step toward socialist transformation is a denial of common sense and a threat to civilization. Just as China's landlords, steeped in Confucian tradition, equated civilization with the peaceful collection of land rent from docile peasants, and so considered land reform a wild attack on all that was sacred and worthwhile, so modern monopoly capitalists, steeped in the Protestant ethic, equate civilization with private ownership of the means of production, and consider the expropriation of private property and socialist transformation to be a savage attack on all that is good and holy, an attack on human nature itself. Many of today's big bourgeoisie are just as unconscious in their class prejudice as China's landlords of old. It nevertheless shines through their every word and act.

But to return to the original argument, the American experts' thesis is, that there was, in fact, no organized opposition, no enemy against whom Mao could mobilize the masses of the Chinese people. It was Mao himself who was rocking the boat and creating one problem after another, one crisis after another, by refusing to accept and support the perfectly normal rational progress which China was making.

Actually it was the intellectual leaders of the opposition in China who gave our American experts this line. Teng To, a leading official of the Peking Party Committee, and author of a series called *Evening Chats at Yenshan*, wrote in his essay *Amnesia* that Mao was a man who suffered from loss of memory. He didn't realize that the Great Leap Forward was a disaster, and he continued to foist his "general line of socialist construction" on an unwilling and exhausted population. "Such a person," said Teng To, "must promptly take a complete rest, must not talk or do anything. If he insists on talking or doing anything he will make a lot of trouble." If Mao failed to take this advice the treatment should be "hitting the patient over the head with a special club to induce a state of shock." So wrote Teng To, and the American experts, responding with enthusiasm, have taken up the cry and repeated it in a thousand variations, which all boil down to: "Dogmatists, revolutionary fanatics, leave society alone, leave the experts alone, leave the people alone. Let them develop the economy along rational pragmatic lines, with due regard to material incentive, to the selfish nature of humanity, to the profit motive."

This is, of course, a call to take the capitalist road, and the all-out support which apologists for American capitalism gave to the opposition forces in China was an indication that the latter were, in fact, the "Party people in authority taking the capitalist road" that Mao said they were.

What posts, what seats of power, did these "capitalist roaders" hold? Even the most cursory survey indicates that they held many key positions in the Communist Party, the government, and the army, not to mention the industrial system, agriculture, education, and culture. Some fairly comprehensive summaries have been made by acknowledged CIA analysts in such publications as *China Quarterly*. One should not place too great reliance on their figures because they are based on information about removal from office which may not be final. That is, during the course of the Cultural Revolution and the many "left" and right swings which it went through, many people were attacked and removed from office only to win support later and return to power at one level or another. It is doubtful whether the CIA analysts have been able to adjust their lists to keep abreast of all these changes. Nevertheless, since they always come forward first and with the most data, their summary is probably more accurate than any other available to us. In any case one may gain some idea of the strength of the "capitalist roaders" from it.

According to these CIA estimates, "capitalist roaders" made up at least two-thirds of the Political Bureau of the Central Committee of the Chinese Communist Party and about one-half of the Central Committee. They led all the regional bureaus, held three-quarters of the provincial governorships, and headed three-quarters of the provincial Party Committees. The President of the Republic, Liu Shao-ch'i, the Secretary-General of the Communist Party, Teng Hsiao-p'ing, the Chief of Staff of the Army, Lo Jui-ch'ing, the man who replaced him, Yang Ch'eng-wu, Marshal Ho Lung, head of the All-China Sports Commission, and a number of other important commanders were leaders of this group, as were Lu Ting-yi, head of the Propaganda Department of the Communist Party, Chou Yang, deputy head of the Propaganda Department, and vice-premiers T'an Chen-lin who was in charge of agricultural work under the State Council and Po Yi-po who headed the State Planning Commission. The mayors of Peking (P'eng Chen), Shanghai (Ts'ao Ti-ch'iu), Tientsin, Wuhan, and Canton were also capitalist roaders, as was Lu P'ing, president of Peking University. Many other university presidents, factory directors, and even commune chairmen turned out to be capitalist roaders. This is, then, quite a formidable group. Just to name the names does not give the whole picture because some of these men wore more than one hat. Liu Shao-ch'i, for instance was not only the President of the Republic but had long led the Organization Department of the Communist Party which put him in a position to place key supporters in Party posts all over the country (a member of the Liu faction, An Tse-wen, took over this job later). Liu also long dominated the trade union apparatus of China. Lo Jui-ch'ing was not only Chief of Staff but concurrently a member of the Military Affairs Commission of the Central Committee and a member of the Communist Party secretariat. He had formerly been Minister of Public Security and had commanded all public security forces.

Since these people were removed from office the CIA analysts conclude that they were part of the opposition, but at the same time these analysts, along with most other American experts, deny that they were an organized group, that they knew each other, communicated with each other, or constituted a faction or headquarters as is alleged in China. Yet if they were not an organized faction it would be difficult to explain the coordination of attack and defense which marks the rise of the opposition before the Cultural Revolution and the massive concerted action which these individuals engaged in at each major turning point afterward.

For instance, when Teng To wrote his essays *Evening Chats at Yenshan* for the Peking *Wanpao*, the *People's Daily* and the paper *Frontline*, they were followed and backed up by another essay series, *Notes from Three-Family Village*, written by Teng To, Liao Mo-sha and Wu Han together, and published in *Frontline*. This Wu Han was none other than the vice-mayor of Peking and the author of the play *Hai Jui Dismissed from Office*. This play and the essays all centered around the dismissal of P'eng Teh-huai as Defense Minister in 1959, and constituted a concerted campaign by one of the most powerful and strategically located Party Committees in China to reverse P'eng Teh-huai's dismissal, bring him back as Defense Minister, and substitute his political line for the line of Mao Tse-tung. Behind Wu Han, Teng To, and Liao Mo-sha stood P'eng Chen, mayor of Peking and a member not only of the Central Committee of the Communist Party but of the Political Bureau of the Party as well.

The play *Hai Jui Dismissed from Office* was ostensibly about an emperor and his prime minister Hai Jui. The message of this play was that Hai Jui was a good man, an official concerned about the welfare of the people, and that he should be returned to office and allowed to lead the country. Actually, of course, this play was not about Hai Jui at all, but about P'eng Teh-huai, and the message of the play was that P'eng Teh-huai had been wrongly dismissed by the new "emperor," Mao Tse-tung, that Mao had been wrong and P'eng Teh-huai right, that Mao's decision to dismiss P'eng should be reversed, and that P'eng should be brought back, not only to lead the Ministry of Defense but to join others like him in leading the country.

If this play had been a one-shot affair by one disillusioned official, it could be interpreted as a spontaneous protest of minor significance. But this play was no one-shot affair. In the first place, it was one of a series of plays around the same theme. Another important one was *Hsieh Yao-huan* by T'ien Han. In the second place, these plays won critical acclaim in the official press, were published in leading cultural magazines, and were staged by publicly financed theater groups.* In the third place, these plays and their message were backed up by various essay series such as *Evening Chats* and *Notes*. These essays expanded and embroidered on the theme and opened up many new lines of attack on Mao and the general line for transition to socialism that he had consistently upheld. How can such a broad cultural attack be viewed as uncoordinated and spontaneous?

Take another example: In 1963 Mao launched the Socialist Education Movement in the countryside. It was a movement designed to strengthen the communes by developing socialist consciousness and collective effort. Its target was "those Party people in authority taking the capitalist road" in the countryside. All this was summed up in a ten-point decision that launched the movement. But no sooner had the Socialist Education Movement been launched than Liu Shao-ch'i and others issued a revised ten-point decision that turned the spearhead of the attack against the rank-and-file cadre on the teams and brigades of the communes, and set as the goal "unravelling the contradictions between being clean and being unclean in relation to the four questions (politics, ideology, organization, and economy)." Liu and his followers substituted this new

---

* *Hai Jui Dismissed from Office* was published in January 1961 in the magazine *Peijing Wenyi* (Peking Literature and Art).

directive for the original and warped the movement wherever they held power. To counter this, Mao issued a twenty-three-point statement that placed the emphasis once again squarely on "capitalist roaders" in the countryside and the struggle between two lines, the proletarian line of collectivization and public interest and the bourgeois line of private enterprise and self-interest. It is difficult to see how a major revision of line in a nationwide campaign could be carried out by individual pragmatists who had no organizational links.

A third example may be taken from the Cultural Revolution proper. Soon after the first Red Guard units arose in Peking and Mao met with the militant young rebels in T'ien An Men Square to give his approval to their movement by putting on a red armband, Red Guard units suddenly appeared in widely scattered cities all over China. Strange to say, many of these first units were not rebels at all, but loyalists who defended the people in power in their localities as good Communists and good revolutionaries, as Mao's local representatives. As the struggle developed, new rebel Red Guards arose in many of these same communities; they exposed the first units as reactionary fronts for capitalist roaders in power, often led by the sons and daughters of the very officials who most needed criticism and removal from office. The rapid formation of Red Guard units nationally was thus exposed as a move at cooptation by the opposition. Seeing the threat posed by militant students in the capital, the opposition had quickly organized a tame student movement in the provinces hoping to avoid the thunder and lightning of mass criticism and attack. It is difficult to see how this nationwide response to events in the capital could have been organized by people without ties or links to any headquarters. All the evidence points to the contrary conclusion, that the bourgeois headquarters led by Liu Shao-ch'i was if anything better organized than the proletarian headquarters led by Mao, and tended to move first and fastest at each turning point in the struggle. It was harder for honest rebels to get themselves together than it was for revisionists already in power to create a movement around themselves. More detail on this sort of action and reaction will be given later. For now it is enough to indicate evidence of an organized opposition in China as a rebuttal to the theory of the experts that no such thing existed.

To postulate a bourgeois headquarters in opposition to a proletarian headquarters is not equivalent to saying that everyone who eventually ended up in the opposition was consciously there in the first place, or that everyone who eventually rallied to Mao's support was consciously there at the start. Far from it. Hundreds of thousands, millions of people were educated, saw through the opposition, changed sides, developed politically in the course of the struggle, and this is of course why Mao Tse-tung and his supporters took the issues to the people in the first place.* That urgent issues existed, however, is due to the fact that there came into being in the years preceding the Cultural Revolution a conscious opposition, centered around Liu Shao-ch'i, and that this opposition was organized. During the struggle that broke into the open in 1966 this opposition fought in a sophisticated way to win support, maintain its power, and impose its line on China. Wherever and whenever it was defeated it then tried to create as much chaos as possible, often through ultra-left attacks on whatever new organs of power the people set up, in order to discredit the proletarian headquarters, prevent its con-

---

* In places where new Party Committees have been organized, less than 1 percent of the old Party members have been expelled.

solidation, and thus lay the groundwork for a comeback.

Mao and his supporters called the "Party people in authority taking the capitalist road" a handful. From the foregoing it is clear that this was quite an imposing handful, able to rally some impressive mass support, especially at the start. Is it correct then, to call it a handful? Yes, when viewed in terms of the support that Mao and his headquarters were able to rally during the struggle, it is correct.

At the start, when Liu Shao-ch'i and his right-wing followers still held important positions of power, Mao's headquarters included Lin Piao, Minister of Defense; such Political Bureau members as Hsieh Fu-chih, Kang Sheng, and Ch'en Po-ta; Premier Chou En-lai; Foreign Minister Ch'en Yi; and such important military commanders as Huang Yung-sheng, Hsu Shih-yu, Hsu Hsiang-ch'ien, Wu Fa-hsien, Yang Ch'eng-wu, Liu Po-ch'eng, and Yeh Chien-ying. This group had the support of a quarter of the provincial governors, many deputy governors, many leading political officers and deputy political officers (commissars) in the army, tens of thousands of middle-level cadre, both civilian and military, the rank and file of the army, and millions of students, tens of millions of workers and hundreds of millions of peasants who rallied strongly to Mao's side as the issues became clear. That the masses of the Chinese people wanted to take the socialist road and carry the revolution through to the end was never in doubt. When viewed in relation to these overwhelming forces mobilized by Mao, those adhering to the bourgeois headquarters must indeed be called a handful.*

---

* As the Cultural Revolution unfolded ultra-left trends developed both among the masses and within the leading bodies at all levels. Mao's headquarters underwent several upheavals as important cadre who had united against Liu Shao-ch'i and revisionism split on such issues

as the revolutionary conduct of foreign policy and the role of the army in the mass movement. By the second session of the Ninth Party Congress in the fall of 1970 Ch'en Po-ta was attacked as one leader of a "left" opposition which now appears to have included Huang Yung-sheng, Wu Fa-hsien, and possibly even Lin Piao. But while Mao's original headquarters group split, the same could not be said of the masses of people below who, as "right" and "left" lines were exposed, dissolved their factions in favor of expanding alliances committed to Chairman Mao's line. If by 1971 Mao retained less top-level support, he had won far greater mass support than ever before—and this time it was more conscious and sophisticated than anything that had existed prior to 1966. Thus the "handful" concept still holds. During the Cultural Revolution Mao has been able, as so often in the past, to unite the great majority of the cadres and the great majority of the people behind the main thrust of the revolution.

Chapter 3

Whose Politics Takes Command?

What were the issues that divided the main contending forces at the start of the Cultural Revolution? I have already summed them up in a general way as the socialist road versus the capitalist road, as revolution versus counter-revolution in the guise of modernization, but it is important to make this more concrete, particularly since most American experts deny that there were any such issues. If they admit any real content to the struggle at all beyond a factional dispute over personal power, they claim that the conflict arose over how to modernize China, hence reflected only a contradiction among the people and definitely did not reflect any basic conflict between mutually antagonistic classes over two mutually exclusive roads to the future.

Any survey of the issues that crystallized out of the struggle, however, indicates fundamental differences between the two sides on almost every important question of development and direction in every sphere, whether it be agriculture, industry, education, culture, military affairs, or foreign policy. Take agriculture to start with. The basic issue here was whether to strengthen collective agriculture, moving steadily from lower collective forms to higher collective forms, with the eventual goal of making all land

41

and agricultural capital the property of the whole people, or whether to make concessions to individualism and private enterprise, pander to the lowest common denominator of peasant consciousness and enlarge private plots, expand free markets, reduce planning to the family level, and base production on the family as the unit, thus in effect bribing peasants to produce rather than mobilizing them as revolutionaries to transform their lives, transform nature, and transform the world. These two lines in agriculture were symbolized by two contradictory slogans, the first, "Learn from Tachai," raised by Mao Tse-tung, and the second, "Learn from T'ao Yuan," raised by Liu Shao-ch'i. Tachai was one brigade of a commune in a rocky and eroded part of Shansi Province, that with a spirit of self-reliance, and without aid from the state, transformed its hills and gullies into fertile fields by cutting stone, laying up walls, and carrying in earth. This transformation was carried out through collective effort after protracted political education and in the course of constant struggle against individualism and private-profit mentality. The result was a gradually rising standard of living for all members of the brigade, expanding sales of surplus grain to the state instead of demands for relief, the accumulation of reserves against bad years, the reconstruction of most of the housing in the village, and the establishment of many community projects to serve the people and community industries to supplement agricultural income. Tachai also pioneered in doing away with the work-point system learned from the Soviet Union, where every job done by every member has to be recorded and rated, substituting in its place an annual appraisal of the working capacity of each brigade member based on criteria that reflect collective consciousness and the ability to work well with and lead others in common projects. This represents a major break with direct material incentive and has released productive potential that ordinary material incentives have been unable to tap.

T'ao Yuan (Peach Garden) was a brigade in a commune on the plain in East Hopei where natural conditions favored intensive production and high yields. Singled out by Liu's supporters for special aid with the idea that capital investment there would show remarkable results, this brigade had little to show in the long run.* Early high yields could not be consolidated. Morale fell and so did political consciousness. In the face of difficulty the membership demanded help rather than mobilizing themselves for all-out effort. Having placed machines and technique above man and his consciousness, T'ao Yuan cadre led the peasants down a blind alley where reliance on material incentives led to disunity, quarreling, and apathy.

One way to sum up the differences between the Tachai road and the T'ao Yuan road would be "politics in command" versus "technique in command," reflecting a fundamental difference between the approach of Mao Tsetung and Liu Shao-ch'i on the whole question of agricultural development. Mao insisted that in China cooperation must precede mechanization while Liu Shao-ch'i insisted that only after China's economy as a whole had developed to the point of being able to provide machinery, fertilizer, insecticides, and other vital products could the peasants form viable producers' cooperatives, or, in other words, that mechanization must precede cooperation. Liu's theory holds that productive forces—land, technique, machinery, and labor power—determine productive relations—the arrangements men make for production—

---

* Liu's wife, Wang Kuang-mei, actually led the Socialist Education Movement in T'ao Yuan.

and the whole superstructure of ideology and culture that follows as a result. Mao, on the other hand, understood that the connection between productive forces, productive relations, and superstructure is dialectical and in constant interaction. Sometimes one aspect is decisive, at other times another. While the forces of production play a major role in determining the contours of human society, there are times when new productive relations are needed to release and develop new productive forces, when changes must be made in the superstructure to bring about changes in the base, times when consciousness determines being, rather than being determining consciousness. At such times massive political transformation is a prerequisite for further productive development.

Quite obviously here we have a fundamental difference that applies not only to agriculture but to the whole of the economy and to the whole of the superstructure of Chinese society as well. If politics must take command in agriculture in order to build socialism, if one must rely on the former poor and lower-middle peasants to carry through a revolution in productive relations and in consciousness in order to develop the productive forces in agriculture and lay the groundwork for an advanced socialist society in the countryside, so politics must take command in industry and one must rely on the working class to transform all productive relations in industry together with the consciousness of all workers in order to release the enormous productive forces latent among the people and thus likewise lay the groundwork for a socialist society in industry. Public ownership of mines, mills, and factories may very closely resemble private ownership and in the long run will lead back to some form of new class control if the internal relations between managers and workers, between technicians and bench- or assembly-line workers, and between workers themselves are not transformed. Socialism is not simply a question of modern technique and large-scale production; it involves the radical transformation of every kind of human relationship, of human motivation, of human consciousness; it involves the release of the enthusiasm, the energy, and the creativity of the masses and the development to the fullest of the capacity of each individual. Efficient, modern mechanized production alone will not lead to socialism. Only revolution can do that. Efficient, modern mechanized production alone will not release the full potential of the masses in production either. Only revolution, only socialism can do that.

It should be stressed here that Liu Shao-ch'i's "technique in command" does not mean the *absence* of politics. It means the supremacy of the old politics, of bourgeois politics, as opposed to the supremacy of revolutionary or proletarian politics. This is because, if one stresses only technique and forgets class struggle, if one tries only to transform productive methods and not productive relations and consciousness, the productive relations and consciousness which will develop will be capitalist, will be bourgeois. It follows that "technique in command" is not some alternative way to build socialism but a way of building capitalism. And since in the modern world the capitalist road is truly barred to any underdeveloped nation by the overwhelming power of already developed imperialist states who will not allow any new capitalist centers to develop but only satellite economies, this bourgeois road can only lead back to semi-colonial, semi-feudal status for China or any other developing nation.

"Politics in command" versus "technique in command" has also been expressed as the opposition between being "red" and being "expert." Here too one must not fall into the trap of thinking that "expert" means without politics.

There is no such thing as an expert without politics and if he or she does not have revolutionary proletarian politics he or she has reactionary bourgeois politics. "Let the experts lead" means, in fact, let capitalism develop, because experts with capitalist consciousness cannot develop anything but capitalist relations of production and a capitalist superstructure to match it. One important problem facing China as Mao sees it is to turn bourgeois experts into proletarian revolutionaries, and to turn proletarian revolutionaries into experts so that all may be both "red" and "expert"; it is impossible to relax and say, as one of Liu Shao-ch'i's supporters is reported to have said, "Whether the cat is white or black makes no difference so long as it can catch mice," which means: "It makes little difference what ideology our technicians have so long as they increase production."

Liu Shao-ch'i's policy of "technique in command" led directly to a dependence on advanced foreign technology; this in turn led, paradoxically, to a slowdown in China's own rate of advance. Those who see technique as central often suffer under the illusion that it is necessary to go abroad to beg, borrow, or steal the latest creations of others. Such attitudes, in so far as they were applied, put China and the Chinese people in a very passive position. Chinese-made products, Chinese initiative, and Chinese creativity were downgraded in favor of slavish worship of everything foreign. Instead of putting people to work developing new products and advanced designs, Liu Shao-ch'i advocated sending away for them.* When they arrived, even if they did not fit the Chinese situation, Liu's lieutenants forbade tampering with them on the grounds that

---

* The slogan in shipbuilding was: "It is better to buy than to build, and better to rent than to buy."

China's scientists and technicians were too backward to improve on foreign technology. This question of whether to depend on foreign technology or to seize the initiative and create new, advanced products suited to China became very important in the Cultural Revolution and stands today as one symbol for the difference between the two lines and the two roads advocated by the opposing factions. Numerous examples of the progress made in industry and agriculture once this fetish of foreign superiority was smashed have been cited by the Chinese press. That the whole problem is directly linked to the problem of whether socialism or capitalism is to be built in China is quite obvious. The socialist revolution must be self-reliant, for no imperialist or social-imperialist state will help China build socialism. If most technique must come from abroad, then the price for its importation cannot but be a retreat from socialism into some form of modernization approved by the technically advanced. Furthermore, if one relies on imperialists and social-imperialists for advanced technique one must also rely on them for the management, marketing, and educational trappings that surround it. Modernization comes in a complete package and it carries a bourgeois label.

Self-reliance not only opens up the socialist road, it also makes rapid advance possible by bringing the creative power and enthusiasm of the whole people into play. To import technique and hedge it round with all manner of rules and restrictions is a slow way forward as compared to giving the people their head and allowing them to take command of production.

Liu Shao-ch'i's policy of "technique in command" also helped to insure the domination of education by bourgeois intellectuals who stressed technical competence above class stand, personal careerism above serving the people, the superiority of things foreign over things Chinese whether new or old, the absolute domination of foreign dogma over conclusions drawn from direct investigation and study of living phenomena, examinations as surprise attacks on one's ability to memorize over real tests of one's ability to learn and to reason, theory over practice and the separation of theory from practice, cultivation of the sons and daughters of the old and new elite over developing the latent ability in every worker, peasant, and revolutionary intellectual—in short, Western-style bourgeois education over proletarian socialist education, the goal of which, according to Mao Tse-tung, must be to "enable everyone who receives an education to develop morally, intellectually, and physically and become a worker with both socialist consciousness and culture," so that each can truly serve the people instead of serving his or her self-interest, his or her career.

Education and educational policy became one of the central issues of the Cultural Revolution, and not without good reason, for the question of the future of any revolution is very directly tied to the question of "revolutionary successors," as Mao so aptly named the young generation that must eventually take over, and the consciousness of these "revolutionary successors" will in large part be molded by the education they receive. It became clear in the late fifties and early sixties that the bourgeois intellectuals who dominated most schools were training up a new generation in their own image. Only a vast shakeup of the whole system, the basic re-education of most teachers, and the development of a completely new curriculum and new methods for the integration of study, work, research, design, and production could transform Chinese education into socialist education capable of creating cadre both "red" and "expert." It seems clear that in this field, too, there is more involved than simply two methods of modernization. Bourgeois education has brought and can bring a measure of technical progress to undeveloped countries, but it cannot bring them to socialism. Socialist education is something as qualitatively different from bourgeois education as socialism is from capitalism.

Education is, of course, only one aspect of the cultural superstructure. The two lines of the two opposing headquarters set contrasting goals for every aspect of it. Some of the sharpest struggle occurred in the theatrical field, especially in regard to opera, which is far and away the most popular art form in China. Literally millions of people participate in the production of various operas and hundreds of millions watch them, learn parts of them, sing operatic arias, and mimic operatic gestures. Liu Shao-ch'i's supporters in the cultural field, while giving lip service to the reform of classic opera and to the need to create new works, in practice supported endless revivals of old operas and created not a single new work. It was Chiang Ch'ing, Mao's wife, who persisted in operatic experiment and inspired a few small troupes to create major new works like *Taking Tiger Mountain by Stratagem* and *The Red Lantern* that express the spirit of socialism. Chiang Ch'ing was also responsible for the reform of the great modern opera *The White-Haired Girl* and its conversion to ballet.

That *The White-Haired Girl*, an opera about landlord repression and peasant revolt conceived in Yenan in the new democratic period, should need reform may puzzle those readers familiar with it. Did it not, after all, describe revolution using stage techniques unprecedented in the Chinese theater? The answer is that *The White-Haired Girl* reflected the revolutionary consciousness of bourgeois intellectual writers and performers in the new democratic period. Though it was anti-feudal and anti-imperialist overall, it gave expression to many bourgeois sentiments, including opportunism, that became obvious to a new generation of opera lovers with firsthand experience in socialist revolution.

In the original version, a young peasant girl is surrendered to a landlord to settle her father's debt and only starts to fight back when the landlord fails to marry her. Pregnant by him, she is sent to work in the kitchen, while he arranges a match with another wealthy landlord's daughter. On the eve of the wedding she runs away, hides near a temple in the mountains, bears her child without help, watches the infant starve to death, and almost dies of hunger herself. Hardships turn her hair white. In the end her childhood fiancé returns as an Eighth Route Army soldier, and leads the people of the village to settle accounts with the heartless landlord.

In the new version the girl never allows the landlord to rape her. She fights back with all her might from the very beginning, and, after escaping the lustful squire's clutches, flees to the mountains where hardships unconnected with pregnancy cause her hair to turn white. This version makes much more sense to China's young revolutionaries. After all, if Chinese peasant girls had accepted slavery and rape en route to marrying landlords, no revolution would ever have occurred. Militant peasants did not make deals with landlords, they fought them and liberated themselves in the process. In this new version petty-bourgeois romanticism has been replaced by revolutionary romanticism, but it was accomplished only after sharp ideological struggle with cultural representatives of another trend who muddled up class issues and thus prepared the ground for the capitalist road.

In the field of military affairs two lines likewise emerge.

P'eng Teh-huai's policy of "technique in command" put the emphasis on building a modern professional army after the pattern of the Soviet Red Army, relying on the most advanced technique and engaged full-time in perfecting it. To build a professional army means to develop a corps of professional career officers. The traditional way to do this is to establish a whole system of special training, special privilege, special status, and special tradition for officers who become specialists in modern mechanized war. In contrast to this, Mao and Lin Piao insisted on "politics in command." Lin Piao developed his thesis of the Four Firsts: As between man and weapons man takes priority, in military training political education takes first place over technical training, in political training ideological questions take precedence over routine political problems, and in ideological education the living ideas in people's minds take precedence over the abstract ideas in books. Once Lin Piao assumed responsibility for the armed forces in 1959 he reversed the trend toward professionalism. Officers' uniforms and officers' privileges were eventually done away with. All army cadre regardless of responsibilities served periodically in the ranks and were subject to criticism and supervision by the rank and file. Military training continued at a high level but political work among the people and participation in production again became an important part of army life. In China today the army is a powerful productive force helping on many fronts to push forward socialist construction. In the Cultural Revolution it once again became a key political force directly mobilizing civilian units large and small to carry out Mao Tse-tung's proletarian line. Around the army as core a vast popular militia was again created and China prepared to fight a defensive, people's war as the main form for any coming conflict with imperialism or social imperialism.

Once again, it is clear that these two military lines are not simply two variants on the road to modernization, but have an important bearing on whether China is to build socialism or not. In military affairs as in the field of economy or culture "technique in command" does not mean the absence of politics. What it means is that the army should leave politics to others. This is the classic bourgeois line of "theirs not to reason why, theirs but to do and die." The "technical" army is built as the instrument of whatever class force is in power. Though made up of workers and peasants, such an army can be used against workers and peasants by any class in control of the state. If the officer corps does not consciously struggle to acquire and express proletarian politics, it will automatically develop bourgeois, even feudal, politics and will throw its support to bourgeois class forces as they struggle to take control. If the rank and file do not consciously grasp proletarian revolutionary politics they cannot recognize the basic class nature of their officers or the political direction in which they are being led. The only guarantee that the army and other defense forces will remain revolutionary and support socialism is the political consciousness of the masses of workers and peasants who make them up and of the officers drawn from their ranks. "Politics in command" means proletarian revolutionary politics in command, it means that the first duty of the military is to master Marxism–Leninism–Mao Tse-tung Thought.

P'eng Teh-huai's "technique in command" also meant dependence on foreign military technique, which meant making a deal with some modern industrial power for atomic weapons, rocketry, jet planes, radar, naval ships, etc. As in the case of the economy one must pay a price for the importation of technique and that price, in the long run, must be the socialist road, for neither imperialism nor social imperialism will help a revolutionary country build socialism. Mao's policy of self-reliance did not mean the absence of modern technique, far from it; it meant that China, in order to stand on her own feet, must develop her own atomic weapons, her own rocketry, her own jets and radar, her own naval vessels. This of course meant time and sacrifice, but it was the only policy that could lead to socialism in the end.

The conflict over foreign policy that came to a head in the Cultural Revolution was directly linked to military policy. If, in order to get modern weapons a deal was necessary, this deal could only be made with the Soviet Union. Khrushchev, when approached, was willing to help China with nuclear armed rockets, but he demanded that they remain under the control of Russian troops based on Chinese soil. This amounted to a demand for veto power over China's strategic defense, a power which in time could be developed into veto power over China's whole foreign policy. In addition to bases Khrushchev demanded that China follow the Soviet lead in foreign policy, join the USSR in a deal with American imperialism for the division of the world and in trying to hold back or prevent the revolutionary upsurge in the Third World. Since the national liberation wars of the Third World were regarded by Mao Tse-tung as the main challenge to American imperialism and their progress as the main guarantee that the United States would not and could not launch a third world war, to make such a deal with the Soviet Union meant not only to betray the oppressed people of the Third World but to greatly enhance the possibility of world nuclear war. On this, as on so many other issues, Liu opposed Mao.

Some people will find this analysis hard to accept because of the leading role Liu Shao-ch'i played in the debate and negotiations with the Soviet Union. The exposure of Soviet revisionism is associated by many Westerners with Liu Shao-ch'i. Actually, while Liu did publicly attack the revisionist policies of the Soviet Union, behind the scenes he worked hard for a deal and urged the Chinese Communist Party to go slow in breaking with Moscow because of the danger of war with the United States.

Obviously the differences between Mao's proletarian headquarters and Liu's bourgeois headquarters were fundamental and irreconcilable. They came to a head in the middle sixties for a number of reasons: (1) the rapid development of China's economy and with it the development of bourgeois elitism and the profit motive; (2) the consolidation of revisionism in the USSR and the political support which the Russian Communist Party, with its enormous prestige, gave to likeminded elements in China; (3) the mounting pressure of American aggression in Asia which made basic military and foreign policy decisions impossible to postpone; (4) the emergence of two lines sufficiently sharp and clear for the Chinese people to grasp them and do battle over them; (5) the inability of the Chinese Communist Party to lead the country forward while split into two irreconcilable factions. "The tree would prefer calm, but the wind refuses to subside," a line from an ancient Chinese poem quoted by Mao, aptly sums up the situation. China's revolutionaries would have preferred to continue building socialism calmly but class struggle developed in intensity as China moved forward. In 1965 and 1966 the opposition pushed toward a showdown. Mao and his supporters faced it head on.

Chapter 4

Attack and Counterattack

What form did the struggle take?

If one disregards the clashes of the early sixties, some of which have been mentioned earlier in this essay, the Cultural Revolution proper can be said to have begun with an article in the Shanghai *Wenhuipao* on November 10, 1965, entitled "On the New Historical Play *Hai Jui Dismissed from Office.*" It was written by Yao Wen-yuan, a Shanghai cadre, with the help of Mao's wife, Chiang Ch'ing, after P'eng Chen and the Peking Party Committee had refused to launch criticism of this play written by the vice-mayor of Peking, Wu Han. After Yao Wen-yuan's article came out in Shanghai, P'eng Chen and the Peking Committee went even further, forbidding the Peking press to reprint the article and not allowing Shanghai reprints to circulate in the capital. Nevertheless, the article was reprinted in Peking in the *Liberation Army Daily*. This started a nationwide debate. Attempts by the Peking Party writers to channel debate away from the political heart of the matter—the play's attack on Mao Tse-tung and its defense of Marshal P'eng Teh-huai's right-opportunist line—into an academic discussion of the historical merits of Hai Jui himself were countered by further articles by Yao Wen-yuan exposing the essays jointly written by Wu Han, Teng To, and Liao Mo-sha in *Notes from Three-Family*

Village and by Teng To in *Evening Chats at Yenshan.*
Yao also exposed these writers' shallow attempts at self-criticism as they tried to avoid the political consequences
of their earlier all-out attack. Though these articles and
the debate engendered by them laid the groundwork for
the subsequent dismissal of the Peking Party Committee,
this first round amounted, on the surface at least, to a
mere skirmish in the press and in the colleges, with barely
a hint of the great mass battle to come.

The second initiative on the part of Mao and his supporters was more decisive. This was the big-character
poster put up by Nieh Yuan-tze, a cadre of the Philosophy
Department at Peking University, and six of her colleagues
on May 25, 1966. They asked why mass public debate on
the question of Wu Han's play and the Peking press had
been suppressed at Peking University. These young teachers blamed Lu P'ing, president of the University and
secretary of its Party Committee, directly and by name, for
diverting the struggle into an academic debate. "Was it
not you who personally 'guided' the comrades of the law
faculty to consult 1500 volumes of books and material running to 14 million characters to study the question concerning the 'reversal of wrong verdicts' by Hai Jui?

"By 'guiding' the masses not to hold big meetings, not
to put up big-character posters, and by creating all kinds of
taboos, aren't you suppressing the masses' revolution, not
allowing them to make revolution and opposing their revolution? We will never permit you to do this!"

Lu P'ing's immediate reaction to this attack was to mobilize large numbers of students to attack Nieh and her
colleagues as renegades and counter-revolutionaries who
openly attacked the leaders of the Communist Party in
their institute. For a week the rebels at Peking University
were surrounded and isolated by students and faculty who

rallied in support of their Party leaders on the grounds that these leaders represented Mao and the Central Committee.

But on June 2nd Nieh's poster was published in the *People's Daily*, the official paper of the Communist Party's Central Committee, and broadcast to the nation by Peking Radio. This led to a tremendous upsurge of the student movement, not only in Peking but nationwide as people rallied to Nieh's call:

"All revolutionary intellectuals, now is the time to go into battle! Let us unite, holding high the great banner of Mao Tse-tung's thought, unite round the Party's Central Committee and Chairman Mao and break down all the various controls and plots of the revisionists; resolutely, thoroughly, totally, and completely wipe out all ghosts and monsters and all Khrushchev-type counter-revolutionary revisionists, and carry the socialist revolution through to the end."

The opposition, taking advantage of Mao's temporary absence from Peking, reacted to this surging student movement by sending in work teams to suppress and divert it. They came with left slogans hardly distinguishable from those of Nieh's call but in practice they suppressed the uprising against university administrators by closing the university gates, turning away the delegations of students, peasants, and workers who were coming to learn from the poster debates, and sending everyone back to their classrooms and dormitories to study Liu Shao-ch'i's *How to Be a Good Communist*, and carry the revolution through to the end by exposing the "reactionaries" in their ranks.* It amounted to a complete about-face designed to protect

---

* The Chinese title of this book is better translated as the "Self-Cultivation of a Communist."

conservative administrators and Party leaders in high posts by setting the masses to fighting one another. This was called "sitting on the mountain watching the tigers fight."

For fifty days work teams organized by higher educational and Party committees dominated the scene in key institutions in various parts of the country but they were unable to break up the rebel groups on several important campuses such as Peking University and Tsinghua University and in the end the rebels exposed them. When Mao returned to Peking they were withdrawn.

Some of the rebel groups took the name Red Guards and it was from their ranks that the nationwide Red Guard movement sprang when Mao met with their representatives, put on a Red Guard armband, and encouraged the youth of the whole country to repudiate and overthrow the "old ideas, culture, customs, and habits of the exploiting classes" and replace them with the "new ideas, culture, customs and habits of the proletariat," to "struggle against and overthrow those persons in authority who are taking the capitalist road, to criticize and repudiate the reactionary bourgeois academic 'authorities' and the ideology of the bourgeoisie and all other exploiting classes and to transform education, literature and art and all other parts of the superstructure not in correspondence with the socialist economic base, so as to facilitate the consolidation and development of the socialist system."

The Red Guard movement, liberated from "fifty days of white terror," as the students came to call the June–July work-team period, mushroomed into an enormous mass movement that soon included almost all the university and high school students in China. But not all of its units and members were rebels by any means. To organize youth into a rebel force was an initiative taken by Mao Tse-tung and his revolutionary headquarters but the op-

posing conservative headquarters, undeterred by the col-
lapse of its work-team strategy, moved quickly to coopt
the Red Guard movement by sponsoring counter-organiza-
tions under conservative leadership everywhere. As has already been pointed out, very often the first Red Guards to
raise a banner anywhere were called into being by the local
Party Committee and led by the sons and daughters of its
leading cadre. Where power was in conservative hands the
role of these Red Guards was to protect the Party Committee from attack, defend the status quo, and intervene,
with their bodies if necessary, to prevent the overthrow of
established authority.

From the names adopted by various units it was impossible to tell which were rebels and which were loyalists.*
The General Headquarters of Red Guards from Shanghai
Schools and Colleges (First Headquarters) early pre-
empted the field in that city. It supported the status quo.
Its affiliated unit at the Foreign Languages Institute was
called the Red Guard Regiment. The Revolutionary Committee of Red Guards from Shanghai Schools and Colleges
(Second Headquarters) united the rebels citywide and its
affiliated unit at the Foreign Languages Institute was
called the Field Army. These groups were for over-
throwing people in power at all levels. Nationwide organizations with such titles as Red Guard Army, International
Red Guards, International Revolutionary Rebel Army,
and the May 16th Brigade turned out to be conservative
while the Peking Red Guards' Revolutionary Rebel General Headquarters (Third Headquarters), the Red Rebel
Regiment of the Harbin Military Engineering Institute,
and the Chingkang Mountain Corps of Tsinghua Univer-

---

* The Chinese word I have translated as "loyalist" is *pao huang*—literally, "defend the emperor."

sity were radical units which established nationwide liaison centers. Some of these later generated ultra-left splinter factions which were rightist in essence, but in 1966 they concentrated their fire on "those Party people in authority taking the capitalist road" who made up the Liu Shao-ch'i faction in power in so many places.

The language used by both rebels and loyalists was all but identical since both sides based their arguments on Marxism-Leninism and Mao Tse-tung's thought and claimed to be champions of Chairman Mao's cause. "What should our attitude be toward people who quote Chairman Mao in support of erroneous ideas? Lenin says: . . . 'Marxism is an extremely profound and universal subject. It is not surprising, therefore, that in the "reasoning" of people who have betrayed Marxism one often comes across a quotation from Marx—usually taken out of context.' " This is one argument from a booklet entitled *100,000 Ways of Looking at Things* compiled not by the rebel Field Army at Shanghai's Foreign Languages Institute but by the loyalist Red Guard Regiment.

When asked by one school administrator if they wanted the leadership of the Party, students at this Institute answered with one voice "Yes!" They did not realize how he had loaded the question. "It sounded as if he were asking 'Do you want the leadership of the Communist Party of China?' In fact he was saying 'Do you believe that we, the Party Committee of this Institute, are worthy of obedience as representatives of the Chinese Communist Party, and more especially, of its leader, Chairman Mao?' Most students, brought up to think of the Party as a monolith, all parts of which were always equally reliable, were in no position to distinguish between the Party as a whole and this particular section of it that controlled their Institute. For them, the Party Committee was still 'Yenan' rather than 'Sian,' still the incarnation of the Central Committee's authority." *

All this made it extremely hard for any rank-and-file person to distinguish right from wrong, true rebellion from false rebellion, and real defense of Mao Tse-tung from fake defense. It was mainly because the conservative groups tried in one way or another to suppress the rebels and this suppression took increasingly raw forms that the rebels were able, in the long run, to expose them.

The struggle between rebel and conservative students soon carried beyond the campuses into the streets, workshops, and communes of China. Rebel groups began to form in factories, in working class districts, and in rural villages. This whole trend was encouraged by Mao and his headquarters and constituted a fourth initiative. It was countered almost at once on a nationwide scale by the formation of worker and peasant units for the defense of the status quo. These also took militant names and preached Mao Tse-tung Thought as their student counterparts continued to do. They won a wide following among rank-and-file people who took their slogans at face value and naturally identified their local Party leaders with the Central Committee and Mao Tse-tung in Peking.

In Shanghai rebel workers built the first citywide organization. It was called the Shanghai Workers Revolutionary Rebel General Headquarters. To counter this Mayor Ts'ao Ti-ch'iu and the Communist Party City Committee helped organize a second movement: The Shanghai Workers Scarlet Guard for Defense of Mao Tse-tung Thought. Starting with a few thousand workers, the rebel organization eventually mushroomed into an army of two million.

---

* Quoted in Neale Hunter, *Shanghai Journal* (Chicago: Praeger, 1969), p. 74.

The conservative organization was large from the beginning. At its peak it also rallied more than a million. Similar developments occurred in Tientsin, Wuhan, Peking, and Canton. Mass demonstrations that brought several hundred thousand onto the streets on both sides began to be commonplace in China's big cities.

One early critical confrontation in Shanghai took place at the offices of the *Liberation Daily,* the official newspaper of the East China Bureau of the Communist Party of China. Some rebel Red Guards and young workers edited a newspaper called *Red Guard Dispatch.* It was printed on the presses of *Liberation Daily* because leaders of the Cultural Revolution in Peking insisted that rebels have access to paper and presses, but it was printed in small numbers and its distribution was left up to the rebel organization. By the end of November 1966 the rebels demanded that *Red Guard Dispatch* No. 8 be printed in editions as large as *Liberation Daily* and distributed along with the latter to all subscribers. This the local Party leaders refused to allow, using as excuse the unwillingness of postal workers to distribute double papers, and the damage to the Party's prestige in the eyes of readers who would tend to equate the two publications. The rebels decided that if their paper could not go out on the same basis as the *Liberation Daily,* then the *Liberation Daily* should not go out either. They occupied the distribution office of the official paper and shut down operations.

This act stirred the whole city. Crowds of citizens, some organized by the Party leaders, others simply upset at being unable to buy a paper or just curious, surrounded the building and blocked the streets leading to it. Organized detachments of workers, who a few days later officially set up the Scarlet Guards, tried to break into the building and drag the occupiers out. The occupiers in turn, threatened by large crowds, called for reinforcements and received them in the form of thousands of workers from the rebel Workers General Headquarters. At the height of the struggle five to six thousand people held the building while tens of thousands milled about outside. One hundred or so who broke in to drag the rebels out were captured and temporarily held prisoner. In the course of the fighting dozens were injured, some by flying glass. Some damage was done to the building and its equipment. But in the main the struggle was ideological. Leaflets, wall newspapers, declarations and statements by loudspeaker and by voice sought to win adherents for each side. According to one rebel account:

> We had only three loudspeakers going, but the opposition had six big ones and drowned us out. Not content with this, they got ten more—brand new they were, with wrapping still on them! They strung the whole eastern end of Nanking Road with speakers, so that we were literally surrounded by noise. This is how they used their material superiority to keep the unenlightened masses from hearing our voice.
>
> Meanwhile our supporters were using propaganda vans to get our views across, but the minute they appeared on the streets they were deprived of their right of free speech. On December 3, about ten comrades from East China Normal College, Futan University, Peking Aeronautical Institute, and the Shanghai Workers Headquarters were surrounded by several hundred people and detained for ten hours. Their big picture of Chairman Mao was taken, their speaker wires were cut, and finally even their van was stolen from them.*

The confrontation lasted eight days. Violence tended to increase as the mobilization on each side escalated, but

---

* *Ibid.*, p. 162.

the political tide definitely ran in favor of the rebels. The longer the crisis lasted the more people heard about it and the more they wondered why rebel opinion should be suppressed. Had not Chairman Mao called for a great debate, for bombarding the headquarters, for exposing the capitalist road everywhere? Had not the Peking *People's Daily* clearly stated that each Party unit must stand on its own merits and could in no way demand to be equated with the Central Committee and Chairman Mao? As these ideas took root, sympathy for the rebels spread, demands to hear their side grew, and adherents flocked to their banner. Though the loyalists did not actually set up their Scarlet Guard until December 6th, the very precision with which they gathered hundreds of thousands of workers into People's Square, ground out leaflets, and issued, on their very first day, a tabloid called *Revolutionary War Express* exposed the hand of the City Party Committee and the established trade union bureaucracy. The whole operation was too well oiled to inspire confidence and rebel forces left no stone unturned in exposing it.

The formal establishment of the Scarlet Guard coincided with a public capitulation on the part of the Shanghai City Committee to the demands of the rebels in the *Liberation Daily* building. Apparently aware that they were losing the political battle, on December 5th Mayor Ts'ao and East China Bureau head Ch'en P'ei-hsien signed an agreement with the Red Guards which specified: 1) their newspaper would be distributed throughout the city with the *Liberation Daily*, copy for copy; 2) the Party Committee of the *Daily* had to act in accordance with the directive from the Central Committee and surrender all "black materials" and photographs it had collected and must be held responsible for all actions in this connection;* 3) the Party Committee of the *Daily* had to make a public self-examination before the revolutionary masses concerning how they had committed grave errors by carrying out the bourgeois reactionary line of the City Party Committee.

The City Party Committee also agreed not to interfere with the revolutionary organizations and their actions, took responsibility for all the consequences growing out of the *Liberation Daily* incident, and guaranteed that no retaliatory measures would be taken against those returning to their posts.

This capitulation by no means ended the struggle. It only shifted the emphasis to a different front. Instead of publicly thwarting the demands of the rebels, Ts'ao and Ch'en agreed to them, but mobilized all the support they could muster to frustrate the rebels in the streets through the mass organizations like the Scarlet Guards which they controlled. No sooner was their agreement with the rebels publicized than the newly created Scarlet Guards publicly denounced it, declared that they had been betrayed by the City Party Committee, and demanded that the agreement be repudiated.

The rebels, however, were not intimidated. They moved to mobilize the support which they had won and forced the City Committee to publicly endorse the agreement which had been signed by two of its members only. An Urgent Notice to this effect was posted on Shanghai's walls on December 8th. Thereupon the majority of the rebels

---

* This was to counter a move on the part of the City Committee to destroy all such materials, thus covering their tracks and burying forever all the best evidence of the reactionary, oppressive nature of their control.

left the *Liberation Daily* building and began to concentrate on mass work to unite and further mobilize the support they had won. In a face-to-face meeting with Mayor Ts'ao they made him sign still another document in which he admitted that he had carried out a bourgeois reactionary line and had provoked the masses to fight among themselves. It was an admission of political bankruptcy. On the following day Workers General Headquarters joined other rebel groups in sponsoring a mass rally attended by over 600,000 people and simultaneously won the mayor's approval for a new publication, *The Worker Rebel*. Both the meeting and the new paper lost no time in making clear the political significance of the recent confrontation, and thereby won still greater support among the masses in Shanghai.

Several weeks of intense struggle followed, during which Ts'ao and Ch'en, in spite of massive defections on the part of their own City Committee cadre, tried to win worker support through the sudden granting of economic demands, bonuses, and retroactive wage settlements, tried to disrupt the economy by strikes and slowdowns and by encouraging thousands of workers, still caught up in the politics of the Scarlet Guard, to go to Peking to air their grievances. Having earlier prevented the rebel workers from going to Peking, and having suppressed rebel activity on the grounds that it disrupted production, they now tried to use strikes, disruptions, and traveling delegations as a club against the Central Committee in Peking, to lay the blame for economic and political chaos on the leaders of the Cultural Revolution nationally and on the local rebels.

In the face of these tactics workers of the rebel General Headquarters took power in plant after plant to keep production going, sent propagandists to the Scarlet Guard strongholds to win over their rank and file, and finally moved to take power in the city as a whole. Their revolutionary committee, made up of representatives from mass organizations of students and workers plus rebel cadre from the old Party organization, held a million-strong mass rally under the leadership of Chang Ch'un-ch'iao on January 6, 1967. At this rally Mayor Ts'ao and East China Bureau head Ch'en were publicly ousted from power. The old Party Committee was dissolved, and revolutionary rebels, primarily workers, took responsibility for China's largest city and main industrial base.

This power seizure, a major turning point in the Cultural Revolution nationally, produced a double response on the part of loyalists everywhere. On the one hand, they unleashed a flood of "economism" throughout the economy, trying to divert revolution and gain popularity with wage increases, bonuses, holiday pay, and travel leave that sharply increased buying power everywhere, depleted public funds, and strained the market with inflationary pressure. On the other hand, they moved to "seize power" on their own account before genuine rebels could organize and challenge them. By dropping a few leading names and raising up a few newcomers from conservative mass organizations they presented local populations and the revolutionary leadership in Peking with a series of *faits accomplis*. New administrations bearing revolutionary names appeared one after the other in widely scattered communities: Tsingtao, Shantung, on January 22nd, Nanchang, Kiangsi, on January 26th, Kweichow Province on January 25th, Kiangsi Province on January 26th, Anhwei Province on January 26th, Shensi Province on January 27th, Taiyuan City on January 28th, Heilungkiang Province on January 31st. Of these it appears that only the seizures in Heilungkiang and Shantung were genuine. A lasting Revolutionary Committee which received approval from Mao's headquarters in Peking appeared in Kweichow one month later. In Kiangsi Province it took another year. In Anhwei the Revolutionary Committee was not set up until April 18, 1968, and in Shensi not until May 1, 1968. Tremendous mass struggles occurred in all these places between January 1967 and the spring of 1968 when revolutionary forces able to unite the majority of the active masses finally managed to take power and consolidate it.

From the outside it looked as if the seizure of power in Shanghai alarmed and alerted the loyalist forces all over the country to a frenzy of activity, as well it might. It was one thing to face debate, wall posters, leaflets, and radical newspapers denouncing this or that reactionary trend and this or that official. Overthrow was something else again. When the "Party people in power taking the capitalist road" saw that the rebels really meant business, meant actually to take power, they used every means at hand to forestall this, including economism and false seizure. They then suppressed rebel action in the name of the new revolutionary committees, even using armed force in some places. In these circumstances Mao and Lin Piao ordered the armed forces to support the revolutionary left not with arms, but politically. In Heilungkiang and Shantung the People's Liberation Army stepped in to arrest and expose the reactionary leaders of the Red Flag Army—an organization of veterans. In other places PLA leaders had difficulty determining which organizations were left and which were right. Mistakes were made. Loyalist organizations gained PLA support in some places and when they were attacked by rebel groups the PLA intervened and was itself attacked as counter-revolutionary. In April the PLA was clearly instructed not to use force in disputes between mass organizations, but to intervene organizationally and politically to support the left, help resolve disputes, and create alliances of rebels and all possible allies. This did not always work.

The Wuhan incident of July 1967 threatened to escalate the whole struggle to the level of armed conflict. Information about this incident is fragmentary, to say the least. So far as I can determine, the facts are as follows: In Wuhan as in other areas mass organizations of rebels came into conflict with established Party authorities and the mass organizations supporting them. Ch'en Tsai-tao, Governor of Hunan, under vigorous attack from rebel students and three organizations of steelworkers from the Wuhan mills had helped organize yet another worker organization called the Million Heroes. When the rebels became strong enough to present a real challenge Ch'en not only encouraged the Million Heroes to physically suppress them, he ordered Independent Division 8201, the local garrison troops under his command, to break up rebel demonstrations and arrest rebel leaders. The rebels defended themselves with arms and serious fighting broke out.

At this point the Cultural Revolution Committee in Peking sent two members, Hsieh Fu-chih and Wang Li to Hupei to investigate the cause of the trouble and work out a solution. After looking into the matter these two leaders severely criticized Ch'en's use of troops against the rebel masses and advised him to work for an alliance between the Million Heroes and the organizations of the opposition. Instead of accepting this advice, Ch'en arrested the two delegates and held them incommunicado. Wang Li was apparently even beaten up.

In this impasse Chou En-lai himself flew down to Hupei to try to settle the affair. As his plane approached the landing field he saw that it was surrounded by large contingents of the Million Heroes plus troops armed with tanks and automatic weapons. Chou En-lai decided not to land

there, lest he himself be arrested and held. Instead he flew
on to another field where troops loyal to the Cultural Revolution Committee were stationed. Then with an army at
his side he drove overland to confront Ch'en Tsai-tao. At
this meeting Chou En-lai arranged for the release of Hsieh
and Wang. Later, after naval units had sailed up the
Yangtze and parachute troops had been dropped at strategic locations around the triple cities (Hankow-Wuchang-
Hanyang), Ch'en himself surrendered and went to Peking
for criticism and re-education.

Apparently this was the only instance where regular
troops in battle array actually faced each other during the
Cultural Revolution. It did not develop into open warfare
because Ch'en's forces were quickly surrounded, and he realized the futility of fighting and surrendered. The mass
organizations that were politically liberated by this sequence of events eventually took part in creating a revolutionary committee to take power in Wuhan and Hupei.

Chapter 5

Consolidating Working-Class Power

Taking power was one thing. Wielding it and consolidating it was another. Various forms of direct mass rule were tried in widely scattered communities in 1967, but the form that won support from Mao Tse-tung and the Cultural Revolution Committee in the end was the three-in-one combination first tried in Shantung and Heilung-kiang in January. This three-in-one combination meant a revolutionary committee composed of delegates from mass organizations, delegates from the old Party organization who were revolutionary or had joined the ranks of the rebels, and delegates from local army units who could back up the new power with the discipline and prestige necessary for authority. Once the three-in-one form won central support the problem locally was to establish a truly representative committee that could unite people against the capitalist road and lead in transforming the status quo in all fields. In most places factionalism engendered during earlier stages of the struggle made such unity precarious. Two tendencies alternately made consolidation difficult. The first was ultra-left. The ultra-leftists having helped to overthrow certain leading figures went on to demand the overthrow of all old cadre without discrimination. Anyone in power was denounced by them as a capitalist roader unworthy of consideration for any post. Under the influence

71

of this line cadre were removed wholesale from their positions. Many rebel leaders, particularly students, mistrusted and attacked all old cadre, regardless of past record or the role that they played in the Cultural Revolution. The second tendency was a reaction to the first. Faced with the wholesale removal of old cadres and the obvious injustice thus done to many good revolutionaries, the demand arose to restore not only the good revolutionary cadres to power, but all cadres to power. From the repressive adverse February current of 1967 which tried to reverse the whole Cultural Revolution and reverse the verdict on Liu Shao-ch'i until today, the Cultural Revolution has tended to swirl between these two poles—from "overthrow all" to "restore all."

Both are counter-revolutionary in essence, though at one time or another they have been supported by large numbers of honest revolutionaries who have temporarily failed to grasp the essence of the matter. It is fairly easy to see that "restore all" would annul the accomplishments of the Cultural Revolution by returning to power not only good cadre but the capitalist roaders themselves. It is less easy to see that "overthrow all" leads in the end to the same result. What the "overthrow all" forces demanded was not only the overthrow of the original Party Committees and government apparatus, but the overthrow of each new revolutionary committee in turn, on the grounds that it contained reactionary old cadre, delegates from reactionary mass organizations, or delegates from army units who were, in fact, conservatives. Had these ultra-leftists had their way, it would have been impossible to consolidate any new power and in the social chaos thus created capitalist roaders could easily have slipped back into effective control. This was so because they were for a long time the best organized, had relatively greater experience in governing and in propaganda work, etc. The same flexibility that enabled a Mayor Ts'ao to capitulate to the rebels and simultaneously to counterattack through mass organizations led by him, would have enabled the loyalists to consolidate power as chaos spread. Thus "overthrow all" and "restore all" turn out to be but two sides of the same coin, the coin of counter-revolution. Before they were overthrown the capitalist roaders tried to crush rebellion. After they were overthrown they suddenly became advocates of complete and absolute rebellion. When the proletarian headquarters reached out a hand to unite with all forces other than diehard revisionists, the latter suddenly came out for restoring all cadre to power on the grounds that no contradictions were antagonistic and that lion and lamb could lie down together and jointly carry through social transformation.

Mao's policy was neither to "overthrow all" or to "restore all" but to mobilize the left, win over the middle, and isolate the diehard reactionaries or, in other words, to unite all those forces that could be united, consisting of at least 95 percent of the masses and 95 percent of the cadres to overcome that handful of Party people in authority who were taking the capitalist road. Such a policy meant educating and welcoming back those cadre who had made mistakes, temporarily followed reactionary leadership and/or temporarily suppressed the masses. This was, of course, no easy policy to follow. How could one tell which cadre had simply made mistakes and meant to reform? How could one tell which cadre were diehard revisionists? There was no easy way to do this. Facts only became clear in the course of protracted struggle. Lin Piao in his report to the Ninth Party Congress quotes Mao as having said: "The problem is that those who commit ideological errors are mixed up with those whose contradiction with us is one between ourselves and the enemy, and for a time it is hard to sort them out."

How complex the situation became is illustrated by the story of Wang Li, the same Wang Li of the Cultural Revolution Committee who went with Hsieh Fu-chih to Wuhan in July 1967. Wang Li returned to Peking a hero. Had he not been seized by a counter-revolutionary governor, had he not been physically beaten, and had he not stood firm throughout, an exemplary follower of Chairman Mao? With his prestige at a high peak he joined with Yao Teng-shan, former chargé d'affaires in Djakarta, who had also been held and beaten by counter-revolutionaries (in this case Suharto's fascists), to lead a "militant" student rebellion in the foreign language schools that were directly under the Ministry of Foreign Affairs. The most "militant" faction of these students was known as the June 16th Group. These student rebels were reinforced by detachments of extremists from the ranks of government cadres. Ignoring the slogan of the Central Committee "Down with Liu, Teng, and T'ao" (Liu Shao-ch'i, Teng Hsiao-p'ing, and T'ao Chu) and substituting for it "Down with Liu, Teng, and Ch'en" (Ch'en Yi, the Foreign Minister), these forces seized the Foreign Ministry itself on August 7th and put Yao Teng-shan in charge. Accusing Ch'en Yi of having conducted a foreign policy of "three surrenders and one extinction" (surrender to U.S. imperialism, to Soviet revisionism, and to domestic reaction, extinguish the flames of revolutionary warfare throughout the world), they proceeded to send directives all over the world that in effect amounted to the export of the Cultural Revolution. Their goal was to turn overseas embassies and consulates into active centers for political agitation against the host governments. Under Wang Li's influence Chinese sailors in Italian ports fought physically with native longshoremen who would not wear Mao buttons. At home, in Peking, British diplomats were beaten up and the British Chancery was burned out in retaliation for the arrest of Chinese newsmen in Hongkong. Top secret archives were broken into and documents known only to a few top officials were made the subject of public wall posters. One rebel student is reported to have remarked, "What's so sacred about state secrets?" Foreign governments reacted sharply to this sudden leftward shift in China's foreign policy and steps were taken by several of China's Asian neighbors to close embassies and consulates and deport diplomats.

Wang and Yao held power in the Foreign Ministry for about two weeks. This was long enough to expose the ultra-left, wrecking nature of their politics. Investigation proved that Wang Li had ties to Liu Shao-ch'i and the capitalist roaders. He was expelled from the Cultural Revolution Committee and detained. Yao and his extremist followers were ousted from the buildings they had seized and the Foreign Ministry was returned to cadres responsible to Premier Chou En-lai. Ch'en Yi did not resume his post as Foreign Minister, but to this day no one has been appointed in his place.* Shortly after this, Chiang Ch'ing, Mao's wife, made an important speech criticizing some Red Guard groups for ultra-left anarchist tendencies, and particularly for seizing arms from Liberation Army depots and attacking army units that they considered to be conservative. Whereas since April, soldiers had been directed to intervene in support of the left, Red Book in hand and without arms, in September they were authorized to de-

---

* After the death of Ch'en Yi on January 6, 1972, Ch'i P'eng-fei, who had served for some time as acting minister, was appointed Foreign Minister.

fend themselves and their equipment with arms if attacked. Such moves as these temporarily blocked the "overthrow all" forces.

It later became clear that these extreme events, the seizure of the Foreign Ministry, the rash of attacks on People's Liberation Army units, and repeated attempts to seize power from revolutionary committees already approved by the Cultural Revolution Committee were all inspired by a secret counter-revolutionary organization known as May 16th after the May 16th, 1966, Directive issued by Mao Tse-tung which launched the inner-Party attack on revisionism. Wherever members of the May 16th held sway they led whatever mass forces they could influence to attack, under left and militant slogans, those solid proletarian forces that had been able to crystallize out of the chaotic struggle. Their ultimate goal was to seize state power in China from the proletarian headquarters led by Mao Tse-tung. Though they never openly attacked Mao Tse-tung himself, rather claiming to be his most fervent supporters, they did repeatedly attack Chou En-lai and other cadres of the proletarian headquarters on whom Mao relied. Though Chou En-lai made clear again and again that Ch'en Yi should be criticized but not overthrown, they overthrew him nevertheless. Most serious of all, they made the People's Liberation Army a main target of attack, seized arms from PLA depots, and launched armed struggle in one province after another. Since it was the PLA that in fact held the country together during the turbulent years, and held it as a proletarian revolutionary force, the attack on the PLA and the persistent efforts to turn political struggle into armed struggle amounted to a direct assault on Mao Tse-tung and Mao Tse-tung's line.

That state power was not an idle dream of May 16th

can be understood when one realizes what important positions were held by key people involved. At least three members of the Central Cultural Revolution Committee, Wang Li, Kuang Feng, and Ch'i Pen-yü, have been named as leaders of the conspiracy. Important military figures, such as Hsiao Hua, head of the Political Department of the PLA, Yang Ch'eng-wu, who replaced Lo Jui-ch'ing as Chief of Staff, Yu Li-hsin, political officer of the air force, and Fu Ch'ung-pi, head of the Peking Garrison Command, have also been implicated. Nor does the trail necessarily stop here. More important people may well be involved behind the scenes.* For the political equivalent of May 16th historically one must look to Leon Trotsky and the ultra-left attack which he launched on working class power in the Soviet Union in the thirties. The neo-Trotskyism of the May 16th Group must be viewed as a counterattack, "left" in form but right in essence, launched by the Chinese bourgeoisie as the right-wing capitalist roaders, who had been the main hope of the class, went down to defeat.

Lest anyone think this is an unwarranted interpretation, consider for a moment the attitude of the American press toward the right and "left" swings in the Cultural Revolution. Reporting on the Red Guard movement which underwent a 180-degree shift can serve to illustrate the point. In 1966 when the main thrust of Red Guard activity centered on the overthrow of conservatives in power, Red Guards were denounced as hooligans, Red storm troopers who were attacking all that was good and civilized in China. The news channels were jammed with instances of Red Guard fanaticism and atrocities. But once a significant portion of the Red Guard, deceived by counter-revo-

---

* See footnote pp. 39–40.

lutionary May 16th elements, went on to attack newly established revolutionary committees that could consolidate
proletarian power, Red Guards suddenly became idealistic
young people whose democratic dreams and aspirations
had been betrayed by Mao. This about-face illustrates how
class-conscious and politically sensitive the American ruling class really is. American radicals and revolutionaries
were, in the main, bewildered by the crosscurrents of the
Cultural Revolution, they were unable to distinguish revolution from counter-revolution when the latter marched
under a red flag. Not so the American ruling class. Its well-
trained experts and journalists sensed very quickly which
flags to support and which flags to attack and they carried
a number of naive radicals with them.

Perhaps the most outstanding example of a sophisticated pro-revisionist line is Neale Hunter's *Shanghai
Journal*, a fascinating day-to-day account of the Cultural Revolution in Shanghai in 1966–1967. This book
contains much valuable information, including texts and
partial texts of hundreds of Red Guard rebel and Red
Guard loyalist wall posters, leaflets, and newspapers, together with a running account of the struggle that enables
the reader to see why and when the various positions were
taken. All this is woven, however, into a background of
subtly expressed bias in favor of the capitalist roaders
while they are still in power, that shifts to strong support
for ultra-left "overthrow all" forces once the establishment
is toppled. To Hunter proletarian revolutionaries are
"Rebels" but right-opportunist counter-revolutionaries are
"Moderates." Ts'ao Ti-ch'iu's bourgeois dictatorship in
Shanghai is pragmatic common sense, but Chang Ch'un-
ch'iao's proletarian dictatorship is minority rule based on
police power and army support. Chang himself is a
"schemer." Shanghai Workers General Headquarters, the

mass base on which Chang Ch'un-ch'iao, with Mao's support, built a new revolutionary power in Shanghai, is consistently downgraded, described as lacking support, losing support, a mere shell composed mainly of outsiders, etc., while Keng Chin-chang's split-off, ultra-left Second Regiment is blown up to large proportions, as a truly mass-based people's movement. When Chang Ch'un-ch'iao's revolutionary rebels attack and criticize conservative officials for handing out largesse in the form of bonuses and wage increases, this is a bad mistake, Chang cannot afford to alienate such key cadre. But when Chang's forces unite with the majority of these cadre and continue them in their posts after criticism, this is unprincipled compromise, the whole Cultural Revolution turns into a charade, rebel youth and workers have been used and betrayed. The essence of Hunter's book is denial of class struggle. All the sound and fury, he avers, comes from a clash between pragmatic communists and dogmatic communists; the result, a healthy shakeup in the bureaucracy but definitely not a transfer of power from one class to another. He pours scorn on the idea that the "extreme left" could possibly have sold out to the "extreme right" of the Party hierarchy, or have any political connection with it, yet this is really the central thread that must be grasped in order to understand not only the Cultural Revolution in China but any revolution anywhere. Hunter takes such pains to throw sand in the eyes on this issue that one must assume method in his stance.

The actual class struggle during the Cultural Revolution in China was certainly complex, even more complex than the classless contention described by Hunter. For that reason it took several years after the first seizure of power in Shanghai for proletarian revolutionaries to establish stable power throughout China. Three-in-one revolutionary committees were formed, failed, and formed again in many places. Mass organizations, rebel and loyalist, united, formed alliances, split, and united again. As established Party committees and governments were overthrown one after the other, the army was often left as the only cohesive social force. The army had to calm serious fighting, strive to bring factions together, arrange to keep production and transportation going, maintain a minimum of social order, support the left and suppress counter-revolution all at once. Though authorized, at least after September 5, 1967, to defend themselves when attacked, soldiers took part in the political struggle unarmed. Many were killed and thousands were injured at various places when they stepped between contending factions to urge discussion and study of Mao Tse-tung Thought in place of violence.

Army cadre, trusted by both sides, often formed the nucleus around which the new revolutionary committees were set up. This has led Western experts to a theory of military takeover. The Cultural Revolution, they claim, ended Communist Party rule and replaced it with military rule. But this is truly obscurantist. The People's Liberation Army (formerly the Eighth Route Army and before that the Workers and Peasants Red Army) has always been an army of the Communist Party in which all leading officers, and a significant portion of the rank and file have always been Communists. From its inception the army has been led by the Party and it has never played a purely military role. On the contrary, army cadre have always played a leading role politically. As far back as 1927 Mao wrote: "The Red Army fights not merely for the sake of fighting but in order to conduct propaganda among the masses, organize them, arm them and help them to establish revolutionary political power. Without these objectives, fighting loses its meaning and the Red Army loses the reason for its existence." From the beginning the army has been the main source and fountainhead of the political cadre that assumed leading roles in the various revolutionary governments that were established. Almost all of the top civilian cadre of the People's Republic of China were formerly PLA commanders or political officers and this was as true of the "Party people in authority taking the capitalist road" as it was of the proletarian revolutionaries who rallied behind Mao Tse-tung in 1966. To replace Liu Shao-ch'i, Teng Hsiao-p'ing, Ho Lung, Po Yi-po, T'ao Chu, P'eng Chen, and their underlings with cadre from the army cannot be interpreted as replacing civilians with military men, since these men were themselves all originally military men. What happened was that revisionists were replaced by revolutionary communists, many of whom owed their political development to their army experience, as did the men whom they replaced. That so many revolutionary rebels emerged from the armed forces can only be explained by the fact that the Cultural Revolution began there years before it began in society as a whole. From the time that Lin Piao took over the Ministry of Defense in 1959 a political rectification began that more or less thoroughly revolutionized the armed forces at a time when revisionist trends were still making heavy inroads on society as a whole.

The final decision as to whether a high-level (provincial, major municipal, or regional) revolutionary committee met the proper criteria for a three-way alliance of revolutionary forces was made in Peking by the Cultural Revolution Group and Chairman Mao Tse-tung. Numerous "overthrow all" and "restore all" committees were formed, held power temporarily, and were later dissolved because they did not meet the requirements established by Mao and his headquarters group. Either they were too far to the left and represented only an isolated group of militants from one small faction or another, or they were too far to the right and amounted only to a reshuffling of the old cadre in power, many of whom were still revisionists. In order to "mobilize the progressive forces, unite with the middle forces, and isolate the reactionary forces" Mao and the Cultural Revolution Group conducted a series of struggles at various levels that were guided by: 1) Concise directives issued by Mao Tse-tung at each turning point in the struggle. Some of these, like "grasp revolution, promote production," were only one line long but they brought clarity to a complex situation such as one in which workers were spending so much time making revolution that their jobs were completely neglected. Mao urged them to both work and make revolution and thus stopped an exodus from shops and plants that could have been disastrous. 2) Detailed articles written by research groups at various levels that clarified the struggle between two lines in one major field after another—first an overall survey entitled "The Struggle Between Two Lines in the Chinese Revolution," then "The Struggle Between Two Lines in China's Countryside," then "The Struggle Between Two Lines in the Economic Sphere," etc. 3) Conferences and Mao Tse-tung Thought study classes in the capital for the leading representatives of various stubborn provincial factions who found it difficult to get together in great alliances or revolutionary committees. 4) Stepping up Mao Tse-tung Thought study classes throughout the People's Liberation Army and calling in models in the study and application of Mao Tse-tung Thought for large gatherings in Peking. 5) Sending high-level People's Liberation Army teams to certain selected government departments, factories, and schools to help solve problems, sum up experien-

ces, and then spread these throughout the army and the
Party. 6) Establishing various Special Case Investigation
Teams to carefully seek out and compile the facts about
leading capitalist roaders in the Communist Party and
their historical role. 7) Establishing cadre schools for the
transformation of the ideology and working style of cadres
from all levels. These were called May 7th Cadre Schools,
were generally established on waste land, and gave officials
long divorced from practical labor a chance to reclaim
land, to plant, tend, and harvest crops, and to build the
buildings they must live in.

This amounted to a tremendous, nationwide educational campaign which drew in more and more rank-and-
file people to debate and contend. Since the opposition
was likewise drawing in people to debate and contend, the
two lines, the two political styles, and the two class forces
gradually emerged with considerable clarity so that hundreds of millions of people could see who really stood for
carrying the revolution through to the end and who stood
for reversing it. This education was tremendously stimulated by the mass printing and distribution of Mao Tse-
tung's works which had hitherto been relatively scarce in
China due to sabotage by Liu's clique. 70,000,000 sets of
Mao's selected works were printed and over 400,000,000
copies of the *Red Book* containing quotations. This gave
everyone a chance to decide for themselves what Mao had
actually said and what it meant.

Revolutionary committees were gradually formed not
only at higher levels, however, but at all levels, in schools,
factories, bureaus, ministries, communes. Here again the
struggle was sharp and prolonged. Factions in the schools
were particularly cohesive and the students and faculty involved found it very difficult to agree on any basis for uniting. In September 1967 Mao issued a statement calling for

grand alliances at every level in which he stated that there was no objective basis for two or more contending factions among workers, no contradiction fundamental enough to lead to organizational splits and endless jockeying for power. Yet the conflicts continued, particularly in the schools. The rebel Red Guards, who had originally opposed and been oppressed by the work teams sent out in 1966 by Liu Shao-ch'i, refused to unite with those loyalist Red Guards who had supported the teams at the time on the grounds that they had followed a reactionary line and forfeited their right to leadership. Those Red Guards, on the other hand, who had, mainly through ignorance, supported the work teams as representatives of the Communist Party and Chairman Mao, could not forgive the rebels for ultra-left "overthrow all" positions taken later. In their eyes the rebels had seriously compromised themselves by counter-revolutionary acts of an ultra-left nature and did not deserve a leadership role either. Two young teachers from England with whom I talked in 1968 said that when they left one of Peking's Foreign Languages Institutes where they had taught for two years, one faction of the students had barricaded itself inside the administration building while the other faction had laid seige to the building and was trying to break in in order to kill those inside.

These differences, so sharply expressed, represented bourgeois or petty-bourgeois jockeying for power and position and were based on the immediate self-interest of the leaders involved, their demands for status and prestige. They were also fanned by counter-revolutionary elements who joined the various factions as activists and promoted "struggle to the end" as a form of social disruption. Students and faculty, in the main, were unable to resolve such conflicts, and it was not until Mao Tse-tung arranged for teams of rank-and-file workers and peasants to move into the schools and take over the direction of the schools, that organizational unity was achieved and effective, functioning revolutionary committees could be set up. These worker-and-peasant teams brought the factions together for the study of Marxism–Leninism–Mao Tse-tung Thought and for exposing and removing counter-revolutionaries who were fanning the flames of factional struggle. They then led the masses of students and cadre in attempts at all-round reform of the schools, the teaching methods, and the curricula. Similar worker-and-peasant Mao Tse-tung Thought propaganda teams were organized to solve problems in urban communities, factories, and farm communes.

Chapter 6

Transformation

By 1969 fairly solid revolutionary committees had been set up at the highest levels in all the provinces, municipalities, and autonomous regions of China. Many good revolutionary committees had also been established at lower levels. Though in most spheres the situation was still very uneven, and though in various places revolutionary committees collapsed or had to be dissolved and rebuilt, the period of power seizure gradually gave way to a period of struggle, criticism, and transformation in the superstructure. Of course one cannot draw a sharp dividing line between these two aspects of the Cultural Revolution. From the beginning people engaged in various forms of struggle, criticism, and attempts at transformation. But when it became apparent that without political power none of this was possible, seizing power became the central task for all revolutionaries, and only after many months of sharp, see-saw struggle did the question of how to use the newly won power for social transformation find its way back on the agenda here and there.

Unfortunately the struggle for power, especially when it broke out into the streets or escalated into open factional fighting, has been much better documented in the West than the efforts at transformation which followed. The American ruling class took a keen interest in the whole

Cultural Revolution when it realized that an important political challenge to Mao Tse-tung and socialist revolution had arisen in China. But as soon as it became clear that Mao Tse-tung and the proletarian headquarters had won a round in Shanghai and were winning one round after another throughout the nation, interest lagged, coverage returned to the status quo ante, that is, to very little or nothing, and all the remarkable changes and innovations that followed were ignored.

This lack of interest leading to a virtual boycott of news about China is one factor holding back understanding of changes brought about by the Cultural Revolution.* Another factor is that the changes are really just beginning, and no overall transformation of the country as a whole can yet be said to have taken place. Numerous social experiments have been initiated and many successes reported in the Chinese media, but as yet the major new forms of education, industrial management, commune organization, etc., have not crystallized, or have not crystallized clearly enough to make generalization possible. I want here to cite only a few examples of the kinds of experiments that have been made in order to suggest the trend. A more detailed summary of the new socialist road will have to be the subject of another study.

In agriculture the socialist road pioneered by the Tachai Brigade has meant rallying the revolutionary class forces, the former poor and lower-middle peasants, overcoming narrow self-interest through study and self-and-mutual criticism, and moving out in a concerted way to strengthen collective ownership, collective production, and collective social services in the face of class opposition from former

---

* This lack of interest ended abruptly with the ping-pong diplomacy of 1971.

rich and upper-middle peasants. One central issue has always been the incentive system which the cooperatives and communes first copied from Soviet experience. What individual team members earned in China's communes was originally based on work points. In order to be fair, work points had to be set for each productive job, taking into account the comparative skills needed, the hardships involved, etc. Then records had to be kept of the amount and the quality of each individual's work from day to day and from job to job. This involved a great deal of record keeping, a great many value judgments, and a great many potential disagreements regarding the relative merits of various jobs and various workers. The system led to a scramble for work points with everyone vying for those jobs where points could be easily earned and slighting those jobs where points were hard to come by. It led to arriving late on the job and leaving early. It led to cadres evolving into straw bosses riding herd on team attendance and quantity and quality of work and keeping endless records instead of joining their comrades in productive labor. All this created contradictions between cadres and peasants, between peasants and their fellow peasants, and between peasants and the state.

At Tachai the whole cumbersome system was scrapped in favor of a method that, instead of measuring the actual work done by each person each day, periodically measured each person as a worker. The basic formula was "work wholeheartedly for the public interest, self-assessment of work points confirmed by public discussion." What this meant was that at set intervals, after a period of hard work, team meetings were held at which each member first said how many points on a scale of ten he thought his work day was worth. The rest of the team then discussed this and if it seemed suitable approved. If it was too high or too low they discussed the matter until a suitable adjustment was agreed upon all around. If a team member set nine points for himself and this was approved by all, then he got nine points for each day worked during the period under review. What these nine points were worth depended on the gross income of the collective for that year, how much grain was sold to the state, and how much grain and money was set aside as a reserve. The total amount left for the people was divided by the total of days worked to get what a standard work day was worth, say $.55 or $.65. A person earning nine points per day would then get nine-tenths of this amount for each of his work days.

At first, in order to provide a concrete standard against which each person could measure himself, Tachai people chose a few models whose progressive ideology, strong labor power, energetic work, skill, and consistent high quality of output were outstanding. With these models earning ten points per day, others could set their points in proportion. Later, after political consciousness had been raised and enthusiasm for collective work had become general, so many people rated model status that comparisons of this sort became invidious. Model choosing was abandoned and the standard work day became a full day's work on the hardest job around. Against this people compared their own efforts, but since this soon led back to a complicated system of recording types of work, this was in turn abandoned in favor of a standard work day calculated at the end of the year after all the crops were in and taking into account all the night shift and emergency work that had been done.

This standard day could be set as high as twelve points but only the very ablest and hardest working members claimed and were confirmed at twelve. Others got 11, 9, 8

or even 4 depending on the consensus of the annual meeting.

This standard work day, "self-report, public appraisal"
system has tremendous advantages for any collective. It
ends the scramble for work points, it ends soft pockets of
privilege, it ends the need for supervision, it ends the need
for complex bookkeeping. It frees cadres for productive
labor. It depends on political consciousness and enthusiasm for the collective to spur hard and careful work and
not on the immediate self-interest of the members.

But of course, this political consciousness and enthusiasm do not fall from the sky. Not every collective can
move right away to such a work-point system. Collective
production must prove its worth in real life, and the value
of putting public interest ahead of private interest as the
central feature of collective production must also be demonstrated. Serious study of Mao Tse-tung Thought is the
starting point at Tachai. What is it that they study? Primarily the selfless attitude of "serve the people" exemplified
by the soldier charcoal maker Chang Szu-teh, the responsible attitude toward work of the Canadian surgeon Dr.
Norman Bethune, and the indomitable spirit of the Fool-
ish Old Man Who Removed Mountains, a mythical peasant undeterred by the greatest material difficulty, who put
man and man's consciousness in first place. The essays
written by Mao on these three men have become part of
the consciousness of Tachai peasants. They help to establish the proper *lichang* or class stand necessary for collective production and the proper attitude toward objective
difficulty. In the old days the peasant response to almost
all problems was *meiyu banfa* (there is no way). Peasants
felt helpless before nature, before the gentry, before life,
and before death. The practice of revolution and the study
of Mao Tse-tung Thought has reversed this formerly pas-

sive attitude with an active *yu banfa*, (there is a way). Thus armed, Tachai people have completely transformed their environment and their lives.

Peasants who study Mao Tse-tung Thought also study *On Practice* and *On Contradiction*, essays on dialectics and dialectical thinking. From these they learn a method, a scientific method, for approaching problems whether political, social, or economic. A peasant who has grasped *On Contradiction* can, like the commune member recently written up in *China Reconstructs*, set himself the task of discovering through the concrete study of concrete phenomena how, for instance, the peanut plant makes peanuts. This peasant doubted the old Chinese proverb, "Once the shoot blossoms the peanut is formed within half a day." He decided to learn exactly what happens when a peanut plant grows, blossoms, and sets its nuts underground, to find out which shoots produce the most blossoms, which blossoms produce the most peanuts, and how cultivation can alter and improve the whole sequence. He sat in the field day and night just watching certain selected plants grow, putting tags on things as they appeared and keeping records of every change. He discovered, among other things, that the first shoots produce the most blossoms and the most nuts, that deep planting weakens or kills the first shoots, while shallow planting threatens germination and hence the very existence of the plant. This contradiction he resolved by planting deep, then removing soil as soon as his seed nuts had sprouted. He also learned to force the first shoots to grow and blossom more by pruning the later shoots. He thus increased the yields of peanuts grown in his team by half. This was the direct result of studying Mao Tse-tung Thought. First he made up his mind to fear no hardship in the service of the people and so set out in wind and rain to complete his observations;

second his grasp of dialectics gave him clues as to what to observe, and what to do about the conflicting phenomena which he did observe.

Since the Cultural Revolution and the mass distribution of Mao's writings, hundreds of thousands, possibly millions of peasants have been drawn into scientific experiment of the type outlined above. The end result of such enthusiasm and effort is difficult to calculate.

In industry the socialist road is likewise based on the transformation of consciousness, on the mass study of Mao's works both as they affect *lichang* or class stand and as they affect *banfa* or method. Material incentive systems with their intense individual competition and bonuses have in the main been scrapped. The relationship between technicians and rank-and-file workers has been drastically altered. Technical innovation has become the business of all participants in a plant or industry, not simply of a few engineers. Research and development is carried on by three-in-one teams of managers, technicians, and benchworkers, all of whom together seek to raise productivity, practice economy, and achieve greater, faster, better, more economical results in the construction of socialism.

"In building up the country we—unlike the modern revisionists who onesidedly stress the material factor, mechanization and modernization—pay chief attention to the revolutionization of man's thinking and, through this command, guide and promote the work of mechanization and modernization." (Mao Tse-tung.)

A concrete example of how this has been done in one plant is given by the Peking Dyeing and Finishing Plant. Before the Revolutionary Committee, composed of rebel workers, technicians, and cadre, seized power, technical practice and technical innovation was in the hands of a few highly trained technicians; afterwards it became the responsibility of the masses. The original technicians, anxious for fame and gain, had studied hard with the aid of foreign books behind closed doors, and had conducted experiments with the aid of a few workers who stood in relation to them as servants to masters. Fearful lest they not be given proper credit for their work, they had kept their ideas and data as secret as possible and shared neither with one another nor with the rank and file. The results were meager. Years of effort and large funds spent on experiments had added a few minor improvements but had definitely failed to revolutionize a production process imported from abroad.

Once the rank and file took over responsibility for technical advance everything changed. The workers decided to begin not from theory and foreign books, but from practice, the actual process of production. Their first move, after thorough discussion, was to speed up the machine that brought the raw cloth into the dyeing process. This speed-up immediately revealed a bottleneck a short way down the line which the workers at that point, with the help of ideas from other sections, tackled and soon eliminated. This brought the cloth at increased speed to a second bottleneck, which the workers there likewise eliminated. By such means, in the course of a few months time, the whole dyeing and finishing process was revolutionized and the production of the plant vastly increased. The old technicians, far from being ignored, were included at every step, first by joining in regular work on the line and second by joining in the consultations to eliminate the bottlenecks as they came up.

Dropping material incentives and individual competition for bonuses and rewards contributed greatly to the results. Any incentive system inevitably builds into a production process a rigidity that makes change difficult. It depends on the high development of specialized skills on a very narrow front and gives various individuals a personal stake in the particular production step and skill which they have developed, thus enabling them to earn more than other people at other spots in the line. In effect a series of "little kingdoms" are created which generate inequality, divide the workers one from another, and foster individualism, technical selfishness, and elitism. Any big change in the process such as a significant increase in the speed of the line and the innovations necessary to cope with it must be resisted by many who stand to lose in the short run. They may have to learn a new job, establish a new rate, and perhaps take a cut in earnings. This is in addition to the fact that the speed-up ordinarily threatens all rates and would, if not accompanied by massive technical change, force everyone to work harder for the same pay.

At the Peking Dyeing and Finishing Plant the acceleration of the line occurred at the suggestion of the rank and file after material incentives and piecework rates had been abandoned. Nobody had any special stake in any special job and all were imbued with the same idea, to do everything possible to increase production to advance socialism in the interest of the whole people. This shift from direct material reward to revolutionary consciousness as a motive force obviously unlocked productive potential that had been suppressed before.

The defeat of Liu Shao-ch'i's "technique in command" line with its emphasis on specialization also unlocked production potential in the area of multiple use. Whereas Liu and the old-style experts had insisted on steel works making steel, auto plants making autos, and refineries refining oil, Mao's insistence on the all-round development of workers and cadre and the all-round development of resources has initiated a campaign for using to the full all the potential of every plant and all its by-products and waste materials. One such success was reported in *Peking Review*:

> Tail gases belching from the chimney of a Shanghai oil refinery used to foul the air. These gases have been transferred to a nearby chemical plant via a two-kilometer-long channel set up by workers who analyzed, separated, and purified them, obtaining ethylene, propylene, and butane from this noxious exhaust. After being synthesized, the gases were transformed into many kinds of chemical materials. They were then delivered to Shanghai's textile mills, plastic and pharmaceutical factories, and machine building plants, which processed them into light, abrasion resistant, and anti-moisture artificial wool, dacron, capron, and other synthetic fiber goods, as well as various plastic goods needed for industry and the people's livelihood, insecticides, medicines, and medical equipment.
>
> By making an all-round and dialectical analysis of the copper, nickel, and acids found in various waste liquids, workers at a small plant . . . created wealth amounting to more than 1.7 million yuan. . . . The copper oxide obtained from such "industrial rubbish" as waste liquids meets the demands for pigment in the country's enamel industry.

Though most enterprises still set one field as their main task they now extend production in other allied or subsidiary fields, wipe out the borderlines between different industries and turn themselves, step by step, into "integrated complexes." A power plant may supply power and produce electrical machinery as a sideline. A machine building plant may turn out both machinery and steel, a steel plant not only steel but machines, cement, chemicals, and chemical fertilizer. "Existing factories have enormous potentialities . . . as long as we boldly mobilize the masses and carry forward the spirit of hard struggle and self-reliance, the workers and technicians, once they start doing the job, can quickly turn out the equipment needed for multi-purpose use. By devoting all our efforts to technical innovations, rational use of manpower, material, and machinery and equipment, ensuring that one man is specialized in one skill and familiar with others, and making one machine do many jobs, we need not add a great deal of manpower, machines, and equipment. Besides, costs can be tremendously reduced by multi-purpose use of waste water, gas, slag, heat and materials in production." The consequences of such recycling and transformation of waste materials for ecology can be enormous.

On the socialist road in China's economy, the Stanford economist John Gurley has this to say.

> In many ways, Maoist ideology rejects the capitalist principle of building on the best. . . . While capitalism . . . strives one-sidedly for efficiency in producing goods, Maoism, while also seeking some high degree of efficiency, at the same time, in numerous ways, builds on "the worst." Experts are pushed aside in favor of decision-making by "the masses"; new industries are established in rural areas; the educational system favors the disadvantaged; expertise (and hence work proficiency in the narrow sense) is discouraged; new products are domestically produced rather than being imported "more efficiently"; the growth of cities as centers of industrial and cultural life is discouraged; steel, for a time, is made by "everyone" instead of by only the much more efficient steel industry.
>
> Maoists build on the worst not, of course, because they take great delight in lowering economic efficiency, but rather to involve everyone in the development process, to pursue development without leaving a single person behind, to achieve balanced rather than lopsided growth. If Maoism were only that, we could simply state that, while Maoist development may be much more equitable than capitalist

efforts, it is surely less efficient and less rapid; efficiency is being sacrificed to some extent for equity. But that would miss the more important aspects of Maoist ideology, which holds that the resources devoted to bringing everyone into the socialist development process—the effort spent on building on "the worst"—will eventually pay off not only in economic ways by enormously raising labor productivity but, more important, by creating a society of truly free men, who respond intelligently to the world around them, and who are happy.*

This, in a sense summarizes the difference between Mao's line and that of Liu Shao-ch'i on the economic front, and makes clear why Mao and the proletarian headquarters were able to generate such vast and enthusiastic support after 1966.

Educational policy, as is indicated in the above quotation from Gurley, is closely linked to industrial and agricultural policy, and during the long period of struggle, criticism, and transformation now underway changes are taking place in education at all levels.

In the countryside the trend is for production brigades to take over full responsibility for primary education. Teachers are no longer selected or paid by provincial or county educational departments but are chosen and supported directly by the brigades, which, instead of paying salaries, award work points to teachers just as they award them to regular members. The new rural curriculum is thus very down to earth, reflecting the practical needs of peasants in production and class struggle. Much use is made of indigenous experts, model workers, and labor heroes, who talk on problems and techniques which they have mastered. Class time is flexible both seasonally and

---

* John G. Gurley, "Capitalist and Maoist Economic Development," *Monthly Review* (February 1971), pp. 23–24.

on a day-to-day basis so that students are free to join production at peak periods. Children can bring baby sisters and brothers to class and even the cattle and sheep which they are tending.

Graduates of these rural schools are expected to stay in their communes and help develop them politically and economically. Those who do go on to higher study such as middle schools in the communes are chosen by their peers for special training which is needed by the community and they too are expected to return home with advanced skills and advanced political understanding that can raise the level of production and class struggle at the grass roots.

The goal of all education, as summarized by Mao Tsetung, is to train "workers with both socialist consciousness and culture" and not intellectual aristocrats who are divorced from revolutionary politics, from production, and from the life of workers and peasants.

Of higher education Mao has said, "It is still necessary to have universities: here I refer mainly to colleges of science and engineering. However, it is essential to shorten the length of schooling, revolutionize education, put proletarian politics in command and take the road of the Shanghai Machine Tools Plant in training technicians from among the workers. Students should be selected from among workers and peasants with practical experience, and they should return to production after a few years of study."

Under the direction of Mao Tse-tung Thought Propaganda Teams from plants and communes the universities and colleges of China are now being transformed along the above lines. Some engineering schools have in effect been dissolved and merged with nearby plants and designing units so that students, teachers, engineers, draftsmen, workers, and technicians rotate through what can be called

urban production communes, producing, learning and creating in turn, and then spinning off production teams capable of setting up new producing and learning communes.

Just as in the rural communes, much emphasis is placed
on the use of advanced workers and engineers in production as teachers in their special fields. These become
part-time teachers on a regular basis. The role of full-time
teachers tends to become one of arranging organic links
between colleges, factories, and scientific research units.
Students may also take the lecture platform from time to
time to share the practical experience which they have,
while full-time teachers must go into plants and rural communes to take part in production.

From primary through all levels of education to the
most advanced, certain key reforms aimed at "producing
workers with both socialist consciousness and culture" are
being introduced. These include: 1) mass education of the
children of workers and peasants, 2) the shortening of
courses with emphasis on quality—"less but better," 3) the
integration of course material with practical work and
manual labor, 4) teaching by enlightenment rather than by
rote, 5) open book examinations that stress ability to find
and coordinate knowledge rather than memorize it, 6) the
living study and use of Mao Tse-tung Thought. These are
not new ideas for revolutionary Chinese. Many of them
trace back to the education pioneered by Lin Piao at Resistance University in Yenan (1937–1945) where students
supported themselves through handicrafts and crop production, teachers and students were equal, gave mutual
help, and practiced self-and-mutual criticism, and study
was closely linked to the practice of the new democratic
society being built there and to the national liberation war
being fought. The village schools of the Liberated Areas

from 1945 to 1949 and the Red and Expert Schools of the Great Leap Forward all were based on these same principles, but the Western style academic instruction, selection through examination, emphasis on expertise and on theory divorced from practice continued to dominate education after the liberation of the whole of China in 1949. More often than not lip service was given to reform while education continued more or less on the old track. All this set the stage for a tremendous upheaval during the Cultural Revolution.

Obviously the rank and file in the mass organizations and the propaganda teams are not having things all their own way. Under sharp attack for traditional practices many students have decided that study is no use and many teachers have decided that teaching is dangerous. When the old discipline collapses a new discipline is hard to establish. Some students become insolent, stay away when they please, and do as they like when they come to school. They even refuse to study on the grounds that they do not want to become targets for re-education sometime in the future. Some parents decide that their children are learning nothing and take them out of school. So many teachers have been attacked as "bourgeois experts" that schools go understaffed. Those teachers who remain are timid, not knowing what to teach and not daring to enforce discipline. Some mumble excerpts from Mao Tse-tung all day long and beg for other jobs where they might earn better wages or more work points. Some peasants in charge of education spend their time sweeping floors and mending chairs. Some factories send sick workers or unsuccessful apprentices to man the propaganda teams, while here and there the factories that run schools find them supervised by teams from other factories who do not relate to their production tasks. This engenders feuds and factional struggles between students, teachers, propaganda teams, and soldiers from the army units who have joined in.

One by one such problems as these are being resolved. They represent not the primary aspect of the reform movement, but a secondary difficulty which can be overcome through political study, through a study of the two lines in education and in social transformation, through honest self-and-mutual criticism, and through practice.

This brief outline of the transformation now under way in agriculture, industry, and education must suffice for the time being. The reader should bear in mind that the struggle for a new, socialist way is spreading to every aspect of life and culture, to military affairs, foreign affairs, advanced scientific research, art, music, literature, and that in all these fields and at all levels most of the issues have not been resolved. Many bold experiments are taking place. While some of them are failing, others are succeeding, and the successful experiences are being publicized to the whole nation and to some extent to the whole world, so that other people may learn from them and adapt them to their needs. For China this is a period of immense ferment and immense creative activity as well as a period of sharp struggle and soul searching.

Underlying all these reforms in society and its institutions is a campaign at the individual level to "oppose self," which is seen as an absolutely essential step in the defeat of revisionism in China and in the world. From an American participant in the Cultural Revolution I received this discussion of the question of "self."

It is impossible for things to go exactly straight. "Left" and right deviations of one kind and another are always cropping up and it is in the fight against these that one's consciousness is raised. They occur in the revolution at large and also in our own thinking. It is as though, for every turn of the revolution, there is a sort of glue that sticks with it. The proletariat tries to remake the world in its image and so does the bourgeoisie. It is inevitable that the bourgeoisie and bourgeois ideology will try to turn every move of the proletariat into its opposite, into something useful for the bourgeoisie. With each move in its struggle to shake itself free from this glue, the proletariat pushes the revolution forward another step. But of course the proletariat will finally shake itself completely free only when we reach classless society and thus when it itself disappears. Only then will the old contradiction be finally resolved and a new one take its place.

The fight against the bourgeois ideas in our own heads, the fight against "self" is much the same. The "self" within us is like this omnipresent glue which persistently tries to twist each of our thoughts into something useful to it. Only by continuous struggle against this glue and constant vigilance as to its tricks can we ourselves keep moving forward on the road to revolution. The enemy knows very well it is the "self" in us which is our Achilles heel, and they will try in every way they can to use this "self" in us to trip us up and lead us astray. This is one of the big lessons I have learned in the Cultural Revolution. To rid ourselves of our own "self" is not merely our own personal task, but also our responsibility to the revolution.

But there is more to this question of "self." It can not only be used by the enemy but is also like blinders on our own eyes. Wherever our subjective thinking starts from self-interest we are blind to the real objective world. "Self" is a formidable enemy in the way of a correct summing up of experience to find out the laws of the objective world. As I see it bourgeois scientists can sum up some of the laws of nature, but not all of them. They can only correctly sum up those which do not affect them personally. As soon as their soul is touched they become blind.

In response to my paragraphs about Mao Tse-tung in the pamphlet *China's Continuing Revolution*, this correspondent goes on to say:

> You have touched on the question of why Chairman Mao is such an admirable revolutionary leader, or, as I would rather say, why he is such a great revolutionary. I think you are right, individual genius is certainly a factor. That is, people are of course not all born with exactly the same ability to think. But as you say, a good brain is certainly not enough to explain Chairman Mao's ability as a revolutionary. It is genius plus the ability to extract from the experience of millions of people in motion (not just in China, by the way, but throughout the whole world) the lessons derived from their actions. —Genius combined with the ability to objectively summarize experience. That is, genius first and foremost without the blinders of "self." This is the source of Chairman Mao's ability.

With hundreds of millions of people "fighting self" in order to "oppose revisionism," mass consciousness in China is on the verge of an extraordinary leap, the consequences of which can scarcely be estimated. No such effort has ever been made anywhere in the world before. One thing is certain, however. It will be that much more difficult for any group to lead China down the capitalist road in the future.

Chapter 7

A Victory for Mao's Socialist Road

What can be said in conclusion concerning the Cultural Revolution?

The first and most important thing is that Mao Tse-tung, Mao Tse-tung's proletarian line, and Mao Tse-tung's proletarian headquarters are winning. One great wave of capitalist restoration that might well have submerged China is being beaten back. China has not changed color. The working class still holds power and the Chinese people are still advancing down a revolutionary socialist road. In the coming period they will strive to transform both the economic base and the superstructure of Chinese society to suit the working class and all working people. And they will continue to inspire and give support to the revolutionary forces of the people of the world in their struggle against imperialism and for national liberation and socialism.

These facts mean that the center of world revolution which once so clearly lay in the Soviet Union, has not only shifted to China but is being consolidated there and is likely to remain there for some time to come. No political force, no political leader anywhere in the world, can ignore this. What happens inside China and what China does on the world scene will increasingly shape the future of all mankind.

One should not, of course, have any illusions that class conflict and two-line struggle have come to an end in China, that working class power is now secure there for all time. In the course of the Cultural Revolution Mao Tse-tung and his supporters, by mobilizing a great mass movement of the people, have confronted one great wave of capitalist restoration. Other waves are sure to follow. It will take decades, perhaps a century or two, before the working class can establish socialism so firmly in any one country that it can no longer be challenged. In fact this can probably only come about when socialism is established on a world scale. One can expect more cultural revolutions in China and many cultural revolutions in other parts of the world wherever working people take power and embark on socialist construction. The experience first of the Soviet Union, and now of China, has established that class struggle continues throughout the period of socialism—that is, throughout the period of transition from capitalism to communism which is a long historical stage —and that far from dying out, it often becomes acute. This experience has also proved that, whereas the working class cannot seize power without armed struggle, the bourgeoisie, new and old, has been able to take back power peacefully by fostering the development of bourgeois productive relations and bourgeois culture and ideology, thus giving rise to a new bourgeois ruling class in an ostensibly socialist state. All this indicates that socialist revolution is much more complex and difficult than most revolutionaries have hitherto supposed, that the seizure of power, which looms so large to a working class under bourgeois dictatorship, is only the first step in a protracted revolutionary process and may well be easier than the steps which follow.

This is likely to be as true of an advanced capitalist society as it is of a semi-feudal, semi-colonial one even though the productive capacity taken over by the working class of the former is of an entirely different magnitude from that taken over by the working class of the latter. In countries like the United States the material problem of the equal distribution of income may well be easier to solve than in China where scarcity continues to be the main aspect of the economy, but the eradication of bourgeois ideology which permeates large sections of the working class, not to mention dominating all other classes, may well be much more difficult. The superstructure created by the American bourgeoisie is complex, sophisticated, many-layered and many-faceted. It will not easily yield to a working class in power, and while the struggle goes on the power of the overthrown bourgeoisie to disrupt, mislead, and attempt restoration in the name of revolution will be great. One must assume a protracted, complicated, and bitter two-line contest throughout the period of socialist transformation. Only a mature and seasoned working class party with a high level of consciousness and a high level of discipline can carry it through.

These are lessons which all radicals and revolutionaries should study.

For American students, many of whom have been influenced and even inspired to action by the revolutionary upsurge of Chinese youth in the last few years the lessons of the Cultural Revolution are fairly clear: students are an important revolutionary force. They are often the first to understand the political issues of their time and the first to go into action. They serve as effective carriers of revolutionary ideas and revolutionary theory, setting political fires wherever they go and galvanizing other people into action. But students as a group, though able to start revolutionary activity, are not able to carry revolution through to the end—that is, they are not able to overthrow bourgeois power and transform society. For this task a great mass movement of working people is necessary. If students fail to help mobilize a broad segment of the exploited and the oppressed and fail to merge their political activity with that of the people they can easily be suppressed and dispersed. If no one takes the trouble to disperse them, they can end up in dead-end factional struggle over what amount to positions of personal power in the student movement.

The Cultural Revolution has also shown that many students are susceptible to ultra-left agitation, much of which is actually inspired by counter-revolutionary wreckers. Instead of undertaking the hard work of uniting all those who can be united against the main enemy of the period, these students rally behind extreme slogans and attack all those who will not join in as running dogs of the ruling class, renegades, or "liberals." Typical slogans of the ultra-left in China are: "Suspect all, overthrow all," "Only the sons and daughters of revolutionaries are revolutionary," and "Absolute equality in everything." Typical slogans of the ultra-left in the United States are: "All nationalism is reactionary," "Negotiation is betrayal," "Only armed struggle is revolutionary struggle," and "The dictatorship of the proletariat now."

Another trend with many student adherents is anarchism. This expresses itself, both in China and the United States, as opposition to organization, discipline, theory, and leadership. Anarchists claim that "all power corrupts" and urge young people to "do your own thing." In confrontation with the organized power of imperialism such concepts have demonstrated their bankruptcy over and over again.

A student movement can make a lasting contribution to

revolution only if it is linked to and serves the working class and all those allied with workers in struggle, and only if it is led by a working class revolutionary party which bases itself on Marxism–Leninism–Mao Tse-tung Thought—i.e., on the accumulated scientific knowledge of all mankind and on the accumulated social experience of the working class in revolutionary struggle throughout the world. Where such a party exists, as in China, revolutionary students have rallied around its proletarian core—that is around Mao Tse-tung and those who follow his line. Where such a party does not yet exist, as in America, revolutionary students should help build one by joining, supporting, and helping to bring together such genuine revolutionary sprouts as the Black Workers' Congress, the League of Revolutionary Black Workers, the Young Lords Party, and the Revolutionary Union. In addition there are local and regional groups not yet linked to any national organization that study and apply Marxism–Leninism–Mao Tse-tung Thought seriously and strive to unite all forces that can be united against the main enemy. These too may be called genuine revolutionary sprouts. They form part of the base from which a national working class revolutionary party may eventually be built.

In China the Communist Party leads a large student movement in the schools and colleges. It also periodically sends students out to work in factories and communes so that they may be re-educated by workers and peasants. After graduation most Chinese students take up posts in basic production units where they join ordinary people in carrying on revolution at the grass roots. In America, revolutionary students should first of all build a strong anti-imperialist movement on the campuses. Whenever possible they should also go to the shops, the plants, and the fields to give what support they can to embattled working people and to help spread anti-imperialist ideas. When they graduate large numbers of students should seek work in basic production and strive, as communist intellectuals, to bring Marxism–Leninism–Mao-Tse-tung Thought to the working class. In order to do this they must live the life that working people live, join in the struggles that working people are actually engaged in, and then help raise these struggles, step by step, to the level of a revolutionary challenge to ruling class power.

In conclusion, I would like to deal with the point stressed again and again by Western "statesmen," Western journalists, and Western scholars. The Cultural Revolution, they say, has greatly weakened China and set it back years if not decades in economic growth, education, and every other sphere that matters. All this, it goes without saying, they blame on that old fanatic, Mao Tse-tung.

Now it is of course true that battles waged by the people of China in the Cultural Revolution have not been fought without cost: five years of massive political struggle involving hundreds of millions of people; the temporary dismantling of large sections of the Communist Party at all levels; serious factional fighting in many places, often escalating wildly from fists and sticks to rifles, machine guns, and even tanks, with casualties in proportion; production disrupted over wide areas for weeks at a time; higher education virtually abandoned for several years and foreign relations suspended or reduced to a bare minimum for the same length of time.

But these temporary setbacks and dislocations cannot be considered a big price to pay for the consolidation of working class power. The fact of the matter is that these five years of conflict have strengthened China, not weakened it. Tempered in bitter battle China's revolutionaries are reuniting under Mao Tse-tung's leadership at a higher level of consciousness and determination than before. It is this consciousness that gives the new unity its strength. The apparent unity of the pre-1966 period, which gave the world an impression of strength, actually covered up a deep and festering split that ran throughout society, stalemated leadership, and frustrated the energy of the whole people. If the question of two headquarters and two lines had not been brought into the open and handled by revolutionary methods the split could only have led to stagnation and disarray, with victory, in the end, going to the capitalist roaders. And since, in the final analysis, no independent capitalist road is open to any underdeveloped country in the age of imperialism, China could only have sunk once again into a state of semi-colonial, semi-feudal decay. It is hardly necessary to repeat here that the opposite is happening. In China the capitalist road back to colonialism is being blocked and the Chinese people are demonstrating on many fronts the vitality and creative power of Mao's self-reliant socialist road.

The ruling classes of the capitalist world are impressed and alarmed.

What else but China's developing unity, vitality, and growth has brought about the complete reversal of Washington's China policy after twenty-one years?

Having done everything in its power prior to 1949 to prevent the Chinese Communist Party from coming to power, the American government set out, after 1949, to bring down the new revolutionary regime through military encirclement, economic embargo, diplomatic isolation, and internal subversion. By 1960 the Soviet Union had joined the United States in this policy. The extraordinary external pressure thus generated on two fronts stimulated and gave support to revisionist tendencies that were already developing inside China as a consequence of indigenous class struggle. As these tendencies grew, both Washington and Moscow took hope and redoubled their efforts.

When the Cultural Revolution exploded American policy makers sniffed victory. What they did behind the scenes we do not yet know. Publicly they threw the whole weight of their propaganda machine behind Liu Shao-ch'i and his clique. When Liu went down, exposed beyond recovery, they rallied behind the ultra-left May 16th Group, but in the end this too was smashed as the American press cried "foul." When the smoke began to clear, Chairman Mao's red flag could still be seen flying over Tien An Men, and all over China millions of determined people rallied to make sure that it stayed there. Clearly in Washington the time had come for a drastic reappraisal.

Nixon asked to be invited to Peking! Behind him the heads of lesser states lined up.

This fact alone is enough to confirm the basic thesis of this essay: Mao Tse-tung and Mao Tse-tung's revolutionary line are winning out in China. In China the working class is beating back the bourgeoisie. In the world revolution of today China leads the way.